CRE**A**TIVE
HOMEOWNER®

the **smart approach** to®

bath
DESIGN

Third Edition

Susan Maney Lovett

CREATIVE HOMEOWNER®, Upper Saddle River, New Jersey

COPYRIGHT © 1998, 2003, 2006

CRE▲TIVE
HOMEOWNER®

A Division of Federal Marketing Corp.
Upper Saddle River, NJ

THE SMART APPROACH TO® BATH DESIGN (3RD EDITION)

SENIOR EDITOR	Kathie Robitz
SENIOR DESIGNER	Glee Barre
PHOTO RESEARCHER	Robyn Poplasky
EDITORIAL ASSISTANT	Jennifer Calvert
INDEXER	Schroeder Indexing Services
COVER DESIGN	Glee Barre
FRONT COVER PHOTOGRAPHY	Mark Lohman; architecture: Abramson Tieger
INSIDE FRONT COVER PHOTOGRAPHY	(top) Minh+Wass; (bottom) Beth Singer; design: Robin Wilson Interiors; architecture: CBI Architects
BACK COVER PHOTOGRAPHY	(top and center) davidduncan-livingston.com; (bottom) Nancy Elizabeth Hill; design: Diane Burgoyne Interiors

CREATIVE HOMEOWNER

PRESIDENT	Brian Toolan
VP/EDITORIAL DIRECTOR	Timothy O. Bakke
PRODUCTION MANAGER	Kimberly H. Vivas
ART DIRECTOR	David Geer
MANAGING EDITOR	Fran J. Donegan

Current Printing (last digit)
10 9 8 7 6 5 4 3

The Smart Approach to® Bath Design (3rd Edition)
Library of Congress Control Number: 2006924700
ISBN-10: 1-58011-318-4
ISBN-13: 978-1-58011-318-2

CREATIVE HOMEOWNER®
A Division of Federal Marketing Corp.
24 Park Way
Upper Saddle River, NJ 07458
www.creativehomeowner.com

dedication

This book is dedicated to the best storyteller I know—my father. He inspired me to become a writer, and he taught me more about remodeling than he will ever realize. Thanks, Dad. I also dedicate this book to my mother, who always encouraged me to capture my thoughts on paper. It's down on paper, now, Mom. Thank you both for everything.

acknowledgments

Thank you to all the people who shared their knowledge and encouragement. I especially want to thank my sister, Melissa, for her daily phone calls to see how the manuscript was coming; my brother, Mark, for his support; my best friend, Julie Peacock, for her unflagging encouragement and help; and my wonderful editor, Kathie Robitz, for her guidance and advice. A special thank you goes to the staff and members of the National Association of the Remodeling Industry (NARI) for sharing your knowledge, especially Bill Carmichael; Chris Miles; Jack Philbin, CR; Jonas Canemark, CR; David Tyson, CR; and Carol Winn—my best sources. Thank you to all the people I have interviewed about home remodeling in the last few years. A special acknowledgment goes to all those readers who relish a long, hot soak at the end of a long day. This book was written for you.

contents

introduction

Twentieth-century literary critic and author Edmund Wilson once said, "I have had a good many more uplifting thoughts, creative and expansive visions—while soaking in comfortable baths or drying myself after bracing showers—in well-equipped American bathrooms than I have ever had in any cathedral."

That was his observation almost half a century ago. How Mr. Wilson would marvel at the innovations that characterize today's bathrooms, such as sumptuous oversized tubs and steam-equipped showers appointed with massaging water jets and multiple sprayers. With **The Smart Approach to® Bath Design (Third Edition),** you'll learn how to incorporate all or some of these features into your own plans.

Given the sophistication of the technology you'll find in today's bathrooms, it's hard to believe that the indoor bathroom is such a recent addition to the home. Even though Queen Elizabeth I boasted of bathing once a month in her sixteenth-century valve water closet—whether she needed it or not—indoor plumbing, in the form of a tub and toilet, has been available to the average homeowner only since the latter part of the nineteenth century.

Today, at least two and a half bathrooms are standard in new construction. For families still faced with the inconvenience of sharing one bathroom, imagine a time when families shared the same tub of water! It wasn't so long ago that water first had to be hand-pumped, then carried to the stove for heating before it was ready to be poured into a tub. Father, the head of the household, was the first to bathe, followed by each of the children. Mother was last. The private bath is a relatively modern concept.

Celebrating the joy of bathing in his 1942 poem "The Sense of the Sleight-of-Hand Man," Wallace Stevens wrote, "One's grand flights, one's Sunday baths." Indeed, bathing should be an indulgent escape, not just a perfunctory hygienic task. However, we are not the first generation to enjoy a therapeutic soak in the tub. Luxurious baths were commonplace centuries ago, with one difference: they were public spaces, not the private ones to which we are accustomed.

As early as the Minoan and the Roman civilizations, the bathhouse was a retreat from the pressures of everyday life, a place of renewal for the body and spirit. Early civilizations combined a variety of features in their bathhouses, but most typically, they consisted of steam chambers, dry heat rooms, and hot and cold tubs with water brought in via terra-cotta pipes or aqueducts. The rooms were often opulently decorated with mosaics, paintings, statues, and intricate architectural details.

Bathing was elevated to an art, and in the process, bathhouses became centers of social activity. In the Roman city of Herculaneum, for instance, the bathhouse included a gymnasium and courts for ball playing; most people went to the baths daily. As the Roman Empire spread to the East, its bathing customs merged with those of the Byzantines and other nomadic people of the area. From that blending of cultures, the "Turkish bath" developed. Bathhouses featured cold and warm baths clustered around a steam chamber, and the experience involved relaxing in a saunalike room, followed by washing, massage, and cooling down.

After the fall of Rome, the use of public bathhouses declined throughout Europe until the eleventh and twelfth centuries. As new cities formed, the ritual of the public bath resurged. Some people also bathed at home in portable wooden tubs filled with heated water, but no real improvements were to come for centuries.

Finally sometime in the late nineteenth century, the bathroom became a permanent, separate room in the home. This change of status was a result of new developments in technology. Indoor plumbing became more commonplace, and people became more conscious of hygiene. Not exactly sure how to decorate the bathroom, the Victorians kept the room functional. Vanities were made to look like pieces of furniture, and claw-foot tubs, favored for their easy access to the plumbing, which was unreliable, abounded.

By the 1920s, the bathroom was a gleaming monument to efficiency. The closed-in, porcelainized tub had replaced the clawfoot version, and the streamlined look of the pedestal sink made furniture-like vanities outdated. Truly luxurious bathrooms of this period featured separate, built-in showers instead of shower-bath combinations. The biggest news in the bathroom was color. White and bisque were still favorites for fixtures, but porcelain could be tinted in pastels, navy blue, or red. Although more stylish, the bathroom was still viewed as functional, not as a haven of relaxation.

Today, the bathroom has come full circle. Over the past couple of decades, the American bathroom has evolved from purely a necessary room to an at-home retreat for pampering oneself luxuriously. It is an amalgam of twenty-first-century technology and Old World refinement. Taking its cue from the centuries-old spas of Europe, the modern bath incorporates features that have been engineered to enhance relaxation and please the senses. And while doing so, good old Yankee ingenuity has made this room safer and more efficient to use, as well as handsome to look at in any price range.

If you are contemplating remodeling an old bathroom or building one that is entirely new, the most important element in creating your perfect retreat is the design. You may be considering hiring a team of professionals to take your desires from the drawing table to reality. Or you may be contemplating doing some of the planning—and perhaps some of the construction—yourself. Either way, you can and should be an active participant in the design phase. For this truly personal space, your understanding and input are crucial to the final outcome.

The Smart Approach to® Bath Design (Third Edition) will help you with all of the aspects of your project. It will give you the confidence to make important decisions about working with professionals, developing a budget, rearranging space, developing a lighting plan, shopping for products, and decorating. It will help you analyze and organize your project just like a designer, walking you through all the steps that are necessary to bring your ideas to fruition. The easy-to-follow Smart Steps will take all the guesswork out of how to go about each phase of the process.

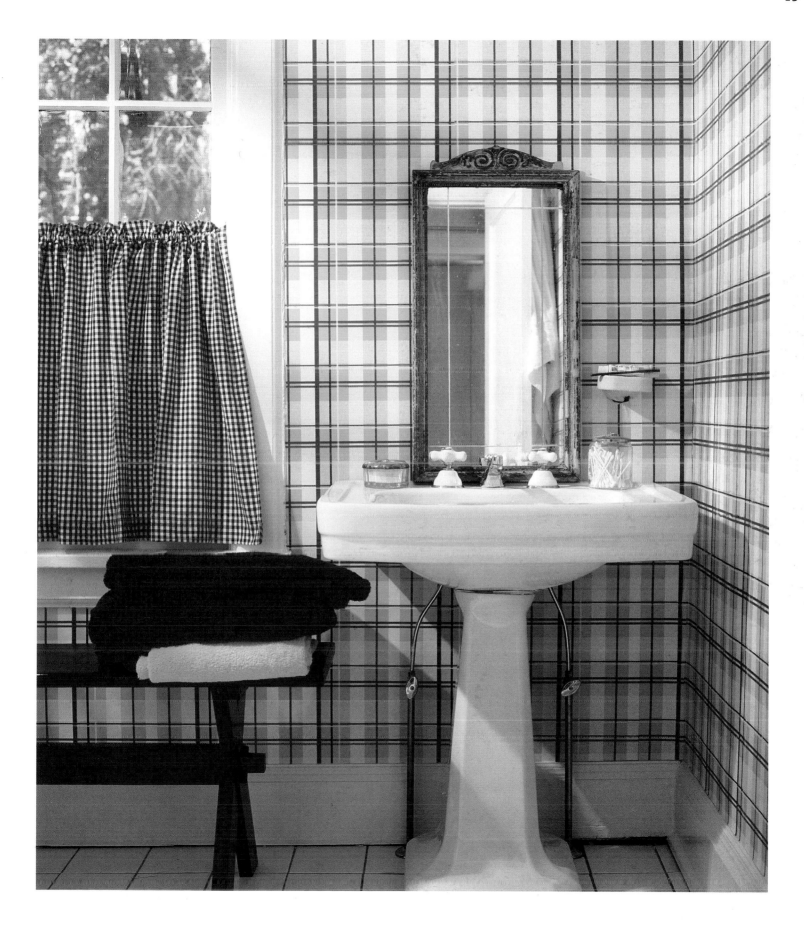

Using this book as a guide, you will feel comfortable relying on your intuition in conjunction with the traditional rules of function and design when you make choices. You cannot ignore the physics of plumbing or the basics of electricity, but you can and should hold your own needs and requirements above what is typical. While your bathroom must have convenient storage, adequate ventilation, and a well-considered floor plan, you'll have to contemplate your special requirements for the room, such as creating separate compartments for the shower, tub, and toilet, perhaps, or incorporating a mini greenhouse or an audio-video center. Today, you can have it all.

This book will help you assess your current bathroom and identify problem areas. It will delve into safety issues and possible future needs. You will discover the basics of design and master ways to include the bath into your home decor. But most importantly, you will learn how to listen to yourself and plan a space that can lull you into a stress-free state at the end of the day or perk you right into action in the morning. Updated and bigger than the original edition, **The Smart Approach to® Bath Design (Third Edition)** will help you approach bath design in the smartest way possible—personally. The finished design will be the best little powder room, sumptuous master retreat, at-home spa, kids' bath, or whatever you need it to be because you conceived it, oversaw its construction, or even built it yourself.

1

smart planning

I f the photographs in this book give you something to dream about, this chapter will give you lots to think about before you ever look at a paint chip or tile sample. You may believe that true contentment comes with a new bathroom in which you can pamper yourself shamelessly. And it may, but the road to making that delightful fantasy come true is full of important decisions about who will actually do the work and what it will cost. It's fine to window shop, comb through books and magazines filled with beautiful pictures, and make lists of all the things you want your new bathroom to be, but you will have to come down to earth for a while and take stock of the big picture. Ultimately, this kind of careful planning is what can make the difference between a disappointing outcome and a job well done.

Large mirrors, well-placed lighting, and a vanity with plenty of storage ensure that this bath will function well.

Committing to a project of this size can be simultane-ously intimidating and exciting. Afterall, it is a major investment of time and money. But don't let your enthu-siasm or any doubts cloud your objectives. One way to remain clear and keep from feeling overwhelmed is to avoid thinking about everything at the same time. Take it easy, and slow down. Do a little homework. Consider all your options regarding who will be involved in the bathroom project and how you will pay for it, one step at a time.

smart steps
call in the pros

■ Step 1 GET THE RIGHT HELP

Redesigning and remodeling a bathroom requires skill and knowledge. In many cases you will need to seek professional help at some point in the project, depend-ing on your particular level of skill. But whom should you use? There are a number of professionals who can assist you. Here is a short list of those who would be qualified to offer advice.

■ **Architects.** If you are planning a significant structural change in your bathroom, an architect is the best choice. While all licensed architects are schooled in design for both commercial and residential environ-ments, one who regularly designs baths for one or two people, versus 30, is the best candidate for your pro-ject. The letters AIA after an architect's name indicate membership in the American Institute of Architects, a national association with local and state chapters that can offer referral services to consumers.

■ **Certified Bath Designers.** Called CBDs, these trained people are certified by the National Kitchen & Bath Association as competent professionals who deal specifically in bath design and remodeling. Because they are specialists, they know the latest in bath prod-ucts and trends and can help you choose the best lay-out and materials for your particular job. (Certified Kitchen Designers—or CKDs—often design bathrooms as well as kitchens and will have them on display in their showrooms.)

LEFT
Unify the bathroom by choosing the same finish for all of the fittings, such as towel and grab bars and faucets.

OPPOSITE
Luxury features in this easily accessible walk-in shower include the adjustable handheld showerhead and a built-in tile bench.

■ **Interior Designers.** Interior designers can help you create style in your new bath and integrate it into the overall look of your home. They do not make structural changes but work with color, pattern, and furnishings to shape a design. You may want to contact an interior designer if you are making significant cosmetic changes to your bath. Some states require licensing by the American Society of Interior Designers (ASID).

■ **Design-Build Remodeling Firms.** These firms retain both designers and remodelers on staff. They are one-stop shops for design help and construction. They are extremely popular because of the convenience of having all of the necessary services within one company. If something goes wrong, you only have to make one call. There is no passing the buck here.

■ **Remodeling Contractors.** Some contractors offer design as part of their remodeling services, or they partner with a design professional. A contractor is a good choice if you have already hired an architect to design the bath or if you are not changing the structure of your bath substantially. To be safe, always work with a licensed contractor.

Whenever you hire people to work in your home, first take the time to research them carefully. Your home is likely your largest single asset. Don't take chances with it unnecessarily. Interview professionals, and follow up on their references. Ask tough questions. Call state agencies and trade associations to check credentials.

Whomever you choose to help remodel the bath will end up knowing you and your family better than your lawyer or doctor. He or she will see you first thing in the morning and after a hard day at the office. That person will be a part of your family for the length of time it takes to complete the project. Check out all professionals as closely as you would a tenant in your home. In addition, take advice from books and magazines. Talk with friends who've been through the process. Clip out articles and photographs, collect notes and ideas, and hit the internet and television shows for further inspiration. Take all of these tidbits of advice and ideas and put them in one place—a dream book, a drawer, or idea box. This is the fun part of remodeling, when you can fantasize and make wish lists of the design elements and amenities that you have coveted for years. That is, until your feet hit the ground and you wake up to the reality of money.

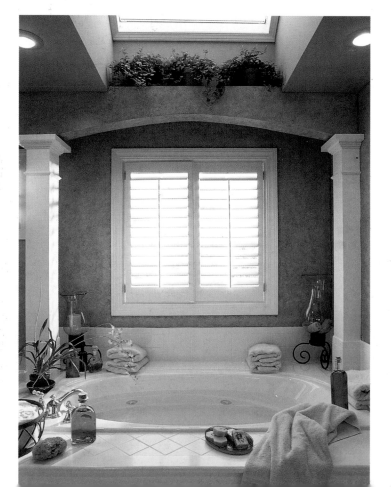

LEFT
For many, the bathroom must include a soaking or whirlpool tub. But do consider whether you'll have the time to actually use it.

BELOW
It's wise to choose neutral colors for permanent elements, such as tile and fixtures, and to add color with art and accessories.

OPPOSITE
When bed and bath adjoin, provide continuity from one space to the other by repeating color, pattern, or materials.

Step 2 ESTABLISH A BUDGET

This is the not-so-fun part of remodeling a bath—finding the money. No one really likes to crunch numbers. Unfortunately, establishing a budget is the only way to determine the size and scope of the project you can afford to design. It is altogether disappointing to plan a luxurious bath, complete with dramatic fiber-optic lighting and a cozy fireplace, only to find that you can barely afford task lighting and a heated towel bar.

Try to avoid paying cash. If it comes down to a choice between paying cash for remodeling or for buying a new car, always go the cash route for the car and finance the remodeling. You can deduct the interest of the remodeling loan from your taxes; you can't deduct the interest on a car loan. Unfortunately, many homeowners will gladly put money up front for a home-improvement project and finance the car. It doesn't make sense.

It also doesn't make sense to set aside money or sign a loan for $20,000 to $30,000 without preparing yourself. How much time would you spend investigating new cars before buying? You would probably read performance reports on various makes and models, then test drive several vehicles before finally making a purchase. Approach a home-improvement loan the same way. Take the time to investigate your financing options.

When seeking estimates from contractors, comparison shop. Use the plans and specifications for your new bathroom to get equivalent bids. If you can't draw them yourself, pay a designer to do it.

OPPOSITE
The painted wainscoting and decorative tub panels, fluted moldings, lighting fixture, and freestanding towel rack give this new bath its timeless and traditional look.

ABOVE
Even a humble powder room can be turned into an elegant space with classic materials such as a honey-toned wood vanity, marble sink, and mosaic-tile floor.

financing

Any bank or lending institution will be happy to tell you how much you can afford to spend on your home-remodeling project. But if you feel more comfortable running a test on your own, here is a quick and simple overview of how banks figure out what you can spend.

The debt-to-income (DTI) ratio

This tells a lender if you can handle more debt on your current level of income. While each lender has its own approved DTI, the average is normally at least 45 percent.

Current monthly expenses	$_____
Add the estimated monthly	
remodeling payment	+_____
Total expenses	$_____
Divide by your gross monthly income	÷_____
This is your DTI	_____%

How to find your maximum payment for remodeling

If your DTI doesn't qualify for financing options, you may need to lower the monthly remodeling expenditure. This calculation will show you how low you need to go.

Gross monthly income	$_____
Multiply by lender's DTI ratio	x_____
Subtotal	$_____
Subtract your total monthly expenses	
(minus the estimated remodeling payment)	−_____
This gives you your maximum payment of	$_____

If the last line is negative, you may have to scale back your plans or do the work yourself on a very tight budget. A negative number means that you won't be receiving funds from a lender. However, you can check out other funding options. For example, a consolidation loan will allow you to incorporate your current debts into your home-improvement loan. Firstly, this will lower the monthly cost of your current debts. Secondly, this loan allows you to deduct the interest from your taxes, something that you can't do on other forms of debt.

Today's financial market offers a variety of other forms of financing as well. You could take out a loan against investments, borrow against your credit card, or the perennial favorite: obtain a private loan from a family member.

Step 3 FAMILIARITY WITH LEGAL ISSUES

Anytime you enter into an agreement, you are venturing into the legal world of a litigious society. Luckily, as one of the contractual parties, you have certain rights. For example, you can change your mind. This is called the legal "Right of Recision." It allows you to change your mind within three days of signing the contract without any liability if the contract was obtained at any place other than the designer's or contractor's office— your home, for instance. This grace period protects you against hasty decisions and hard sells. Federal law mandates that consumers must be made aware of this right to cancel the contract without penalty. Ask your contractor about it before you sign anything.

You should also request waivers of lien, which release you from liabilities for subcontractors and manufacturers. At the end of the job, ask for a final lien waiver for each person who worked on the project to protect yourself from third-party debts and obligations. You don't want to be forced, legally, into paying for a job twice because your general contractor didn't make good on his debts. With a lien waiver, you can refer an unpaid subcontractor to the general contractor for payment. For further protection, ask your contractor for a signed affidavit stating that all subcontractors have been paid.

Furthermore, don't allow anything to happen on your property that is not outlined in writing. If you want a change, get a written "change order." Remember, though, that any change—whether initiated by you or not—will cost more money. It is the nature of the game. Write up every change order with a description of what is to be done and how much it will cost. Always include an estimate of how long the additional work will take to complete and how it will affect the production schedule and project timeline.

LEFT

Plan to include as much storage as possible in your new bathroom. A tall, narrow cabinet, which occupies minimal floor space yet provides a wealth of storage for items like towels and cosmetics, is a smart way to use space.

■ **Step 4** LICENSES, INSURANCE, AND PERMITS

Ask to see the remodeler's license if your local or state government requires one. Call the licensing agent, and verify the status of the license. Just seeing one is not enough. Normally, expiration or suspension notices do not appear on the license itself. You have to call the licensing agency for that information.

All contractors should have current liability insurance and worker's compensation. This insurance covers employees of the remodeling firm while they are working on your property. Make sure that your contractor carries this coverage before allowing uninsured workers to place themselves in potentially hazardous situations in and around your home. If you are still worried about your legal liabilities should an injury occur, talk to your insurance carrier and attorney. You may want your

contracts

You have the right to a specific and binding contract. The more details and pages it has, the better. Get specifics on every part of the project and on every product purchased. It is the details that will save you in the long run. Every contract should include basic items, such as:

■ The contractor's name and proper company name, as listed on the business license

■ The company's address, telephone, and fax number

■ The company's business license number if applicable (Some states don't require licensing. If this is the case, find out the company's business license and verify it.)

■ Details of what the contractor will and will not do during the project, such as daily cleanup around the site, final cleanup, security measures to be taken during the demolition phase, and so on

■ A detailed list of all materials and products to be used, including the size, color, model, and brand name of every specific product (If you have written specifications, you'll need two signatures to change them— yours and the contractor's.)

■ The approximate start date and substantial completion dates during the project (You might ask for estimated completion dates for various stages; for example, one-third, halfway, and two-thirds through the process.)

■ Your signature required on all plans before work begins (This prevents last-minute changes being made without your knowledge and prevents misunderstandings. This way you get a chance to look at the plans one last time before walls come down and cabinets and sinks are placed on the wrong side of the room. One drawback to this provision is that it could cause delays if you are out of town during the renovation or are slow to respond. You may want to provide an address where you can be reached by overnight carrier or designate someone to sign in your absence.)

■ Notification of your Right of Recision

■ Procedures for handling changes in the scope of the work during the course of the project (The procedures should state how change orders will be handled by the contractor. Change orders should require both your signature and the contractor's.)

■ A listing and full description of warranties that cover materials and workmanship for the entire project (Warranties are normally in force for one year, and should be identified as either "full" or "limited." A full warranty covers the full repair or replacement of faulty products, or your money is returned. A limited warranty indicates that replacements and refunds are limited in some regard. Limited warranty restrictions should be spelled out.)

■ A binding arbitration clause in case of a disagreement (Arbitration enables both parties to resolve disputes quickly and effectively without litigation.)

■ A provision for contractor's statements and waivers of liens to be provided to you prior to final payment

Include anything else that needs to be spelled out clearly. Remember: if it isn't in writing, it does not exist legally.

Most importantly, before signing any contract, be sure that you understand all of the components. You have the right to ask questions and to demand explanations. Never, ever, sign an incomplete contract.

insurance agent to review the plans for the new bathroom and adjust your homeowner's coverage during the length of the project.

Never allow work to be done on your home without a legal permit. Permits may require fees and inspections—two things everyone would like to avoid—but they could save you thousands of dollars in the future.

In some states you, the homeowner, are held responsible if work is done without a permit and a problem occurs. Years may go by, but should a tragedy such as a fire occur, your insurance agency and fire marshal will investigate. If the cause is faulty electrical work that was done during your bath remodeling, your homeowner's insurance company can refuse to pay the claim if there is no permit on record. This could be disastrous should the entire house burn down.

ABOVE
An expanse of mirror makes a room seem larger. Double the effect of artificial light by installing fixtures on the surface of the mirror.

■ Step 5 HAVE IT YOUR WAY

It's your house and your money. Don't hesitate to
ask as many questions as you like about any
detail concerning the project. The more information you have, the happier you will be with the
result. This is particularly true when selecting
products or figuring out warranty coverage. Find
out what is and isn't covered by warranties.
Many manufacturers won't honor a warranty if an
amateur fix-it job has been attempted. Avoid dis-
asters by calling your contractor or the manufacturer for guidance about repairs.

Never sign for any deliveries during a job
unless you personally ordered the materials or
are prepared to be liable for them. Signing for
materials is your contractor's responsibility.
Imagine what would happen if you signed for
an incomplete shipment or the wrong-size floor
tiles. You would be responsible for the error.
Don't take chances. Let your contractor shoulder
the burden of tracking down incomplete, incor-
rect, or damaged orders.

Also remember, the people you hire to work
in your home are in *your home*. You have every
right to tell them not to smoke, play music,
curse, or eat inside. You can even tell them
where to park and how to store tools and materials around your home. Of course, don't be
unreasonable, but don't feel put out in your own
home, either. Make a set of rules before the
work begins, and ask the general contractor to
enforce them. If he or she doesn't, do it yourself.
It is a good idea to include your rules as part of
the contract. That way, you'll have some legal
ground on which to stand when making your
demands. In most cases, however, a reputable
contractor will make sure that workers are
respectful of your wishes.

RIGHT
Few older homes boast this kind of space for a bathroom,
but if you're willing to give up an extra bedroom, it could
become a spa-like bath. This one includes two vanities, a
shower with multiple water sources, and an oversize tub.

permits

If your contractor asks you to apply for the permit yourself, refuse. Most jurisdictions consider the person who obtained the permit to be the general contractor and the one responsible for the outcome of the job. The county or building officials in your jurisdiction will come to you if the work is not up to code during the inspection. If these officials have a problem, it is far better to let them talk to a professional.

If you are doing the work yourself, be sure to find out the laws in your particular area. Some types of work require that a licensed professional meet code; many jurisdictions won't accept amateur work on electrical systems, for example, because the result of an error can be tragic.

Whether you use a professional remodeling contractor or not, keep any paperwork related to the permit in your files for future reference.

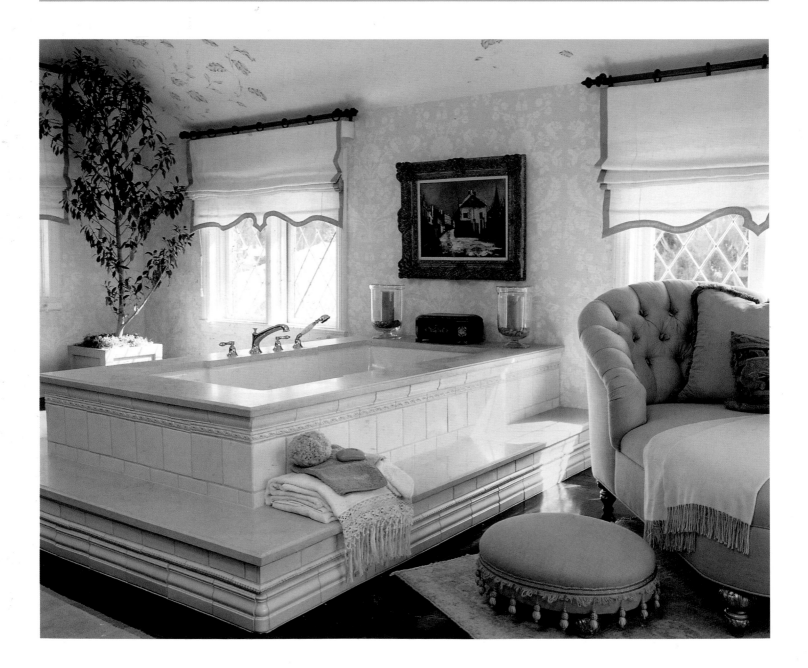

Step 6 TALK THE TALK

Don't let miscommunication come between you and the person you hire. Learn how to make yourself understood. If you are going to remodel, get to know the construction language and jargon. Be sure to check out the glossary in the back of this book for a listing of commonly used terms in bath remodeling.

Decide how you are going to convey problems to your contractor. Again, if you know how you will respond should something go wrong, you won't panic. Are you someone who does not deal well with stress or confrontation? Perhaps someone else in the household could take over the day-to-day communication with the contractor—preferably someone who understands the basic process and can stay calm. Maybe your talents would be better spent in the early planning stages and the final decoration of the room.

Step 7 PREPARE YOURSELF EMOTIONALLY

Remodeling is stressful. There is no way around it, even if you do the work yourself (perhaps especially if you do the work yourself). It's hard to deal with the sawdust, the noise, and the constant inconvenience of not having a working bathroom. At times it will seem as if the project is something that is being done to you rather than for you. But there are ways to ready yourself and your family for the temporary upheaval that could last just a few weeks or maybe months, depending upon how much actual work will be done.

Begin by talking to everyone in the family about what is involved. Discuss any temporary inconveniences all of you can expect and for how long. If there's only one bathroom in the house, you'll have to make plans to stay elsewhere for at least part of the time. Ask your contractor to give you enough warning. If there are going to be

OPPOSITE
Should your new bathtub require steps for access, be sure the flooring material you choose has a nonslip surface.

TOP RIGHT
Wall-hung vanities, which reveal the floor underneath, make a space appear larger and provide a tidy spot to stash a trash can.

RIGHT
The large, walk-in shower features a built-in bench and a recessed niche for keeping soaps and shampoos handy.

strangers in the house, let everyone meet them before the project begins. Your home is your most personal asset and your most private retreat. It is also essential that you and your family know how to protect it and yourselves before there are unfamiliar faces walking in and about your house for an extended period of time.

Contractors often talk about what they call the "remodeling curve"—the wave of ups and downs everyone involved in remodeling goes through. Some days are good (when you see the framing done), and some days are bad (you can't tell whether anything has happened in days). It is normal to experience highs and lows during a project of any size. What helps is to talk about it, expect it, and prepare for it. Decide ahead of time to order out Chinese food or take the kids to their favorite burger joint on those days when it feels as if nothing is going the way everybody would like. Find some way to stave off the frustration. You will feel more in control if you have a plan of action.

Step 8 EVALUATE YOUR DIY SKILLS

Can you do a bath remodel? The National Association of the Remodeling Industry (NARI) offers a quiz to determine whether you should try it yourself or leave it to a pro. Take the test, opposite, to see for yourself.

NARI says if you marked a majority of the answers "yes," you may want to attempt doing it yourself. But before you strap on a carpenter's tool belt, revisit those questions you marked "no." Carefully consider the potential problems you will face in those areas if you proceed with the project. Hiring a professional may still be your best option. Or you may want to use a combination of the two—hiring a professional for the technical and difficult aspects of the job and doing the cosmetic touches yourself. Only you can decide.

For more advice about all of these matters, visit the NARI Web site (www.nari.org). You'll find a homeowner's guide that addresses the most frequently asked questions about remodeling, more tips for financing your project, additional information on contracting matters, and more.

The key is to be honest with yourself. Can you really do this project—or parts of this project—yourself? If so, wonderful. A successful do-it-yourself project can be quite satisfying. If not, then be smart and hire the right professional to help you out. Trade associations like NARI, the National Kitchen and Bath Association, American Institute of Architects, and others are great places to look for top-of-the-line advice.

Finally, if you plan to sell your house any time soon, find out what kind of bathroom amenities buyers expect in your area. A local real estate agent can help you with that information. But whatever buyers want, bringing an existing bathroom up to date or adding the convenience of an extra one is always money well spent. If you do all of the work yourself, you'll probably recoup almost all of your investment. If you hire professionals, expect to get back about 40 percent of what you paid.

LEFT
Pedestal lavatories are an attractive and popular option for today's bathrooms, but they present a unique challenge because they don't provide storage space. Here, the storage issue is resolved with a medicine cabinet that is recessed into an adjacent wall.

should you do it yourself?

Before you make the decision to tackle a bath remodeling project on your own, take a few minutes to answer the following questions. This exercise will help you determine if you have the necessary skills and abilities. Be honest with yourself.

Yes	No	
Yes	No	Do you enjoy physical work?
Yes	No	Are you persistent and patient? Do you have reliable work habits? Once the project is started, will it get finished?
Yes	No	Do you have all the tools needed and, more importantly, the skills required to do the job?
Yes	No	What level of quality do you need for this project? Are your skills at that level?
Yes	No	Do you have time to complete the project? (Always double or triple the time estimated for a DIY project, unless you are highly skilled and familiar with that type of project.)
Yes	No	Will it matter if the project remains unfinished for a period of time?
Yes	No	Are you prepared to handle the kind of stress this project will create in your family relationships?
Yes	No	Have you done all of the steps involved in the project before?
Yes	No	Have you obtained the installation instructions from the manufacturers of the various products and fixtures to determine whether this is a project you still want to undertake? (You can obtain them from most manufacturers before purchase to determine the steps involved in installation and the skill level required.)
Yes	No	Is this a job you can accomplish completely by yourself, or will you need assistance? If you'll need help, what skill level is involved for your assistant? If you need a professional subcontractor, do you have access to a skilled labor pool?
Yes	No	Are you familiar with local building codes and permit requirements? (Check into these matters before beginning work on your kitchen project.)
Yes	No	What will you do if something goes wrong and you can't handle it? (Most contractors are wary about taking on a botched DIY job, and many just won't. The liability is too high.)
Yes	No	Is it safe for you to do this project? (If you are unfamiliar with roofing [for a kitchen addition] or do not have fall-protection restraints, you may not want to venture a roofing job. Similarly, if you know nothing about electricity, leave it to the professionals. Some jobs can have serious consequences if not performed correctly. Your health and safety should be the primary concerns.)
Yes	No	Can you obtain the materials you need? Who will be your supplier?
Yes	No	Are you attempting to do it yourself for financial reasons? If so, have you looked at all your costs, including the cost of materials, your time, and the tools you need to purchase? If you are new to the DIY game, you may also want to consider the cost to correct any mistakes you may make. Will it still be a cost-saving venture given all of these factors?
Yes	No	If you are trying DIY for your personal satisfaction, can you really guarantee a job that will be well done? If it doesn't come out right, how will you feel? Will you need the money to redo any unsatisfactory work? Will you have it? Will you be able to live with mistakes?

design workbook
SPECTACULARLY CLASSIC

timeless classic

Classical elements, such as arches and pillars and natural materials, like stone, tile, and wood, will retain their appeal for decades.

room with a view

Include a window in the tub area only if your privacy will not be compromised and the view is noteworthy. (See also top left.)

convenience feature

A recessed niche incorporated into the wall of the shower provides handy storage for bath products. (See also bottom left.)

storage aplenty

A spacious furniture-quality vanity provides plenty of storage and keeps grooming tools out of sight. Note windows high on the wall, which admit light but preserve privacy. (See also bottom far left.)

design workbook
UPDATED TRADITIONAL

elegant amenities

Gold-tone faucets
and fittings,
graceful lavato-
ries, and wain-
scoting set the
decorative tone
in this bath.

let it rain

A fixed shower
head provides a
rain-like stream
in the separate
enclosed shower.
(See also bottom
far left.)

molding details

Traditional-style
moldings used
throughout the
bathroom lend
the grace of a
bygone era. (See
also top left.)

good grooming

Sconces flanking
the mirrors are
pretty and pro-
vide task light
for grooming.
(See also middle
left.)

match metals

Unify the hard-
ware, fittings,
and the exposed
pipes by using
the same metal
finish. (See also
left.)

2

making space

Master bath, kids' bath, powder room, guest bath—how many bathrooms does one household need? Remember when the typical family shared just a single small bathroom? Times have changed. And although the average family size has decreased, according to the National Association of Home Builders more than 70 percent of the new homes built in the United States in 2004 contained at least two baths; 24 percent contained more than three baths. In this chapter, you'll discover how to make any bathroom functional and practical, starting with making a list of needs and wants, followed by an analysis of the actual space. Once you've done this, you'll be ready to try out different floor plans on paper. Finally, you'll find suggestions for the specific type of bath you want—full-size, luxury, at-home spa or modest powder room.

Many of today's larger, luxurious bathrooms include spa-like features, such as an over-size shower and and a deep tub.

Architect Louis Sullivan said, "Form follows function." That does not mean that style has to be subservient to function, but there must be a balance between the two. Designing a modest bath can greatly increase its performance and your ultimate comfort. Take the time to plan out how you can make the best use of every square foot of floor and wall space.

Whatever the size of your investment, get the best for the money you spend and think about the returns. If you ever decide to sell your house, potential buyers will be put off by cramped bathrooms that look like everything came as an afterthought. On the other hand, you can make a splash—and perhaps a tidy profit—if the fixtures are in good condition, the floor plan appears carefully thought out, the room looks bright, and there is ample storage.

focus on objectives

If you will be working with a design professional, expect to be interviewed at the beginning of the planning stage. He or she will want to get to know you and whoever else will use the new bathroom. Your designer isn't being nosy. He or she simply wants to understand your likes and habits, as well as your basic requirements and greatest expectations with respect to the new bath. Your designer will also make a sketch of the existing space to get an idea of what works and what doesn't. The rough drawing may include any adjacent unused areas that might be considered for expansion.

If you will be acting as your own designer, do the same. You can't assume that you instinctively know what has to be done to transform the old bathroom into a fabulous new space just because you live there. That's acting on emotion. For the best result, approach the project in the same analytical manner as a professional who understands design and can be objective about what has to happen.

RIGHT
The classic lines of the bathtub combined with the black and white mosaic floor tiles give this new space its traditional appeal.

OPPOSITE
A colorful vessel sink, paired with an arched faucet, brings high style to a powder room or master bath.

smart steps
how to get started

■ **Step 1** CREATE A DESIGN NOTEBOOK
It's important to keep all of your ideas and records in one place. Buy a looseleaf binder, and use it to organize everything from magazine clippings to photos of the old bathroom, wish lists, notes and interviews with design professionals, contracts, sample plans, shopping lists, color charts, tile samples, fabric and wallpaper samples, and anything else related to your project. It should be comprehensive yet not too clumsy to cart around to showrooms, stores, or home centers.

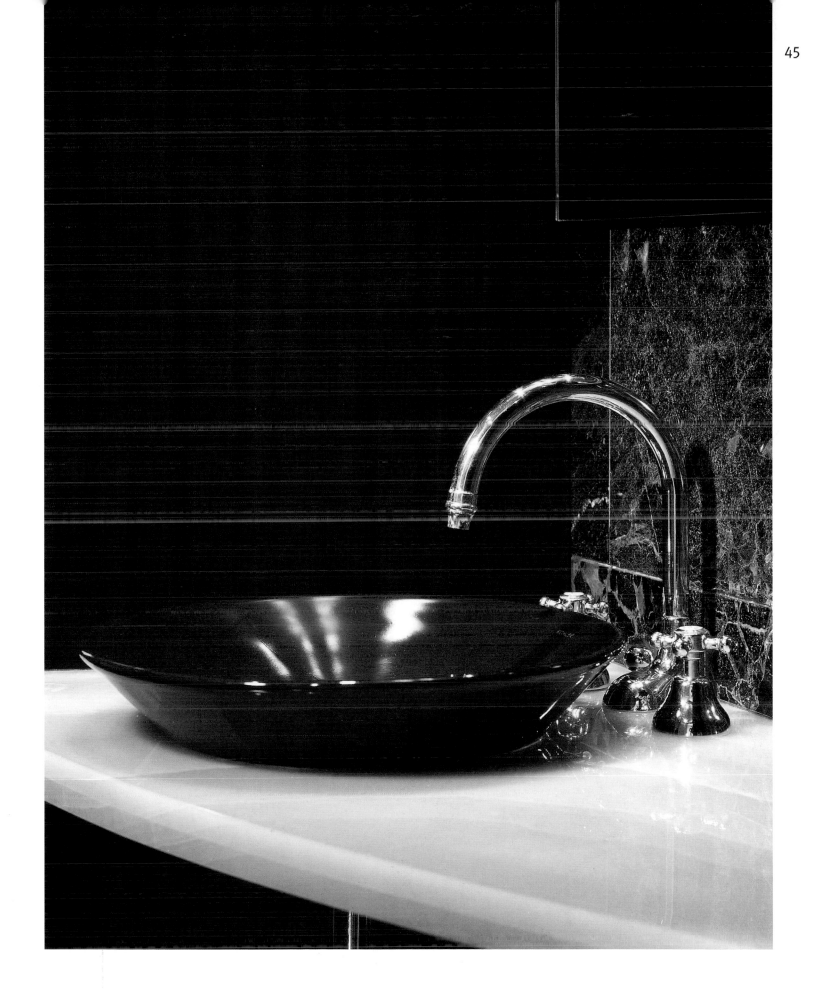

■ Step 2 ANALYZE THE EXISTING BATHROOM

Before you start clipping too many photographs out of magazines, decide what you really want to gain by remodeling. You might begin by asking the most obvious question, "What's wrong with my existing bathroom?" You already know that there's something you don't like about it. Maybe it's just old and outdated. Perhaps it's too small. To decide what you must do specifically to improve the bathroom, ask yourself the kinds of questions any design professional would pose to a client. Record your responses in your notebook.

Begin with, "Who uses this bath on a regular basis?" Jot down bathing preferences. If someone likes a shower instead of a bath, he might prefer a separate unit, with amenities like jetted sprayers, to a whirlpool tub. If the design is part of a master suite, will partners bathe together? A large soaking tub for two may be in order.

Examine the condition of the fixtures. Will you replace all of them, some of them, or none of them? If they are in good condition, you can save money by simply refinishing them. Tradespeople who specialize in recoating enamel fixtures can be found easily in the Yellow Pages.

Does the existing bathroom contain enough storage space? Even if there is a linen closet or cabinetry in the room, it may not be organized efficiently. If you need more storage, make note of it now so that it can be planned as part of the total design.

Also ask yourself whether the fixtures are comfortably situated. Are the sink and toilet installed at the right height for the people who will be using the bathroom? Is the toilet paper dispenser handy? Are the controls easy to use? Are there enough towel racks? Are they easy to reach? There is no one standard prescribed for everybody, and now is the time to get things the way you want them to be.

Make sure to take safety matters into account in your analysis. For example, are there adequate ground-fault circuit interrupters (GFCIs)? Ordinary receptacles can't protect you against the full force of an electrical shock. GFCIs sense an overload in the circuit and cut the current in a fraction of a second. That's faster than your heart beats. Other safety questions to ask include: Is the existing flooring slippery? Is there a tub or shower seat in the bathing area? Can you reach the bath controls from both a sitting and standing position? In addition, the showerhead should have a hand-held unit that is easy to use when sitting or when you're bathing children. And there should be a temperature- and surge-protection device installed with the faucet to prevent scalding.

ABOVE
Hang a large mirror between two wall sconces, and add a shelf below to create a convenient area for quick hair and makeup checks.

OPPOSITE
Choose a vanity cabinet that incorporates plenty of storage. Consider whether drawers or doors will best accommodate what you plan to store there.

Now is also the time to question whether the existing bathroom has enough heat and light. Is it well ventilated? A new bathroom is a substantial investment, even on a small scale, so don't overlook these less glamorous but important aspects of function.

You would be wise to think about maintenance, too. Do existing materials keep you busy with constant cleaning? A black tub may look sophisticated, for example, but it shows every streak of water. Do you want to keep polishing it, or is it worth the cost of replacing it with one that's white or beige?

Finally, if you plan to stay in the house after retirement, evaluate the bathroom layout's potential for accommodating a wheelchair or walker. (See Chapter Three, "Functional Comfort," page 74.) Hopefully, you'll never need either one, but making the changes later may be more troublesome than it's worth.

The answers to these questions should give you a detailed idea about what needs improvement and what may not. If you are adding a bath to the house, the list should alert you to layout and room-arrangement details that may not be your most important concerns but that you also don't want to overlook in your bathroom's design.

Step 3 MAKE A WISH LIST

The design is right when it meets your personal needs and appeals to your senses. Everyone has different habits, individual ways of getting ready in the morning or winding down at night. In fact, some psychologists say that people's hygiene routines will determine how well they sleep and handle stress. If this is true, your bathroom actually may affect your well-being.

Besides basic elements, you may want some special features in your new bathroom. Create a list of all the amenities you would like to include, whether or not you think you can afford them. When you come up with a close-to-perfect plan, look for areas to trim expenses. The money you save may permit a few extras. Suggestions include choosing an affordable laminate countertop and less expensive cabinetry or tilework or keeping old fixtures that are still in good condition.

There are so many options for materials and products nowadays. As you shop, you'll be amazed with

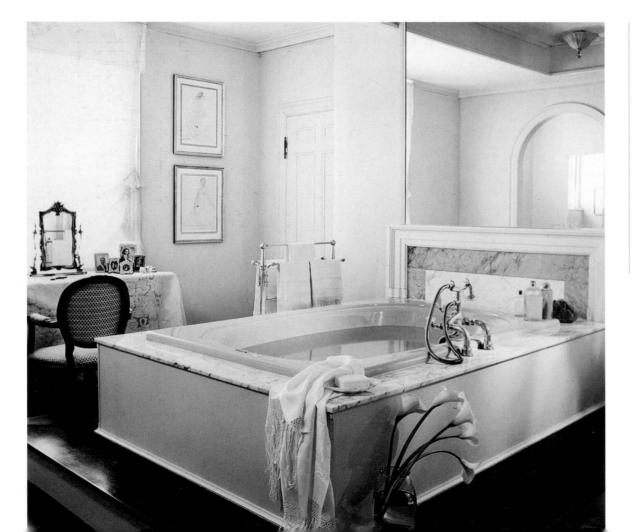

LEFT
This spacious at-home retreat includes many elements that add to the feminine and luxurious mood, including matching gold-toned fittings, framed artwork, and an upholstered chair at the dressing table. But the centerpiece of this space is an oversized tub. The wide deck surrounding it allows for access to the tub.

what is on the market, from basic to luxurious. When you compile your wish list, review take note of everything that fits into your fantasy of the perfect bathroom, in addition to practical features. To make sure your wish list is complete, visit bath design showrooms and home centers. Talk to salespeople who can tell you about new products. Look at manufacturers' Web sites.

Step 4 SKETCH THE OLD FLOOR PLAN

Just like the professional designer, make a drawing of the existing floor plan. First draw a rough sketch, and then transfer your drawing to graph paper with grids marked at $\frac{1}{4}$-inch intervals. This formal drawing of the physical layout of the bathroom is called a "base map" or a "base plan." You can draw it freehand or with a straightedge, but do it to a scale of $\frac{1}{2}$ inch equal to 1 foot.

Start by taking measurements, beginning with the length and width of the room. Then working from one corner, measure the location of all windows, doors, and walls. Record the swing of each door. Note each dimension in feet and inches to the nearest $\frac{1}{4}$ inch. If the

room is small, you may be able to make all the measurements by yourself, but it's easier to have a helper hold the "dumb" end of the measuring tape.

Next, draw the cabinetry and plumbing fixtures, and indicate their heights. Measure the centerline of sinks, toilets, and bidets, and show how far the center of each of these fixtures is from the wall. Be sure to list the overall lengths and widths. Unless the corners of the room are extremely out of square or the walls are leaning, don't worry about small discrepancies in their measurements. Most houses are not perfect. Include symbols for light fixtures, outlets, and heat registers. Make notations for load-bearing walls if you can. Otherwise, consult a trained professional who can tell you whether a wall can be moved safely.

It's a good idea to list your gripes about the old bathroom right on this sketch. That way you can see exactly what you want to change and what you want to keep at a glance. Remember, this map is simply your guide. It doesn't have to be professionally drawn, but it must be accurate in its rendition of the space as it is now to be useful.

ABOVE
Begin by making a sketch of the bathroom as it now exists. Include any adjacent areas that might be used for expansion. Indicate fixtures and electrical and heating features.

ABOVE
Use your rough sketch to create a base plan that is drawn to a scale of $\frac{1}{2}$ inch to 1 foot. This time, be as accurate as possible when indicating measurements.

creating functional space

Whether it's a full-size bath or a powder room, the arrangement of space plays a large role in how well the room will function. A bathroom addition to an outside wall of the house offers the best possibilities for unencumbered floor space. However, it will be the costliest. One way to save money is to bump out the wall by a few feet and extend the existing floor structure out over the foundation. Consult an architect or builder first, to make sure the structure is sound and can carry the additional load. Always inquire about local zoning ordinances that may affect your plans before proceeding. If you violate codes, you could be forced to remove the new construction.

EXISTING BATH

ELEVATION

PLAN VIEW

Bedroom

Bedroom

ABOVE
This elevation and plan show a typical minimum-size full bath between two bedrooms.

NEW BATH

Skylight

ELEVATION

Joist Extensions

PLAN VIEW

ABOVE
Extending the floor joists out a few feet enlarges the space without having to construct a foundation. The original tall window is replaced with a smaller, high window and a skylight.

Can't Add On?

If you can't improve the layout of an existing bath by building an addition, take a good look at areas that are adjacent to the room, such as hallways or unused space under a stairway. Sometimes even a small amount of space stolen from a closet or an adjacent room can be the answer to your problem. If your family requires two bathrooms but there's only enough room for one, forego a spacious master bath for two smaller, side-by-side bathrooms. You'll save money this way, too, because the plumbing lines for both rooms will be right there.

rearranging an existing layout

Y ou may want to modify the layout on paper. A few minor changes in the floor plan can enhance your original arrangement. However, moving plumbing fixtures in an existing bath may significantly raise costs.

smart steps
plan on paper first

■ Step 1 MAKE A NEW BASE DRAWING
Like the base drawing you made for the old bathroom, use a ½-inch scale. If you are using a ¼-inch grid, each square represents a 6-inch square of real floor space. Begin by drawing the outer walls, and then add the windows and doors.

■ Step 2 MAKE TEMPLATES
Paper templates are an easy way to experiment with different layouts. Draw the fixtures to scale on graph paper, and then cut them out so you can move them around your plan. When cutting out templates, include both the fixtures and the required front and side clearances—so you won't get caught short on space. Plumbing codes require a minimum clearance for each fixture. Fixture clearances are shown in the drawings on pages 52, 53, and 55. The top number of each pair indicates the minimum required by code or function. The bottom dimension allows more room between fixtures. Aim for somewhere between the two numbers.

EXISTING BATH

Closet   Closet

Hall

ABOVE
This typical in-line full bath is situated between two bedrooms. Large closets behind the bathroom's walls offer possibilities for expanding the bathroom's size.

BELOW
By expanding into the closet of the bedroom above, there is enough room to include a generous vanity on one side of the room and add shelves to a corner.

NEW BATH

Towel Shelves above Bar

Hall

Step 3 PLACE THE FIXTURES

You will use some fixtures more often than others: first the lavatory, next the toilet, then the tub or shower. An efficient plan places the lav closest to the door, followed by the toilet, and finally the tub, which is located the farthest away. If there is any leeway in your plan, place the toilet so that it will not be visible when the door is open. Even in a small bathroom, the direction of the door swing can help shield the toilet from view. (See page 55.) Another easy way to place fixtures on

ABOVE LEFT AND RIGHT
When planning toilet and bidet placement, use these dimensions to determine the necessary clearances. The bottom number is the preferred minimum clearance. However, if you are short on space, you can use the top dimension, which will not compromise the accessibility of the layout for most people.

ABOVE LEFT AND RIGHT
Use these clearances for rectangular tubs and whirlpools and corner tubs. Try to allow more space than the minimum clearance required by code—the smaller dimension.

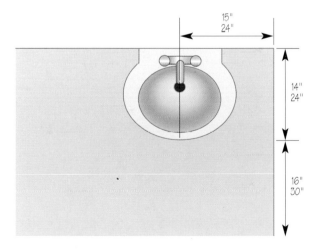

TOP TO BOTTOM

If you don't have a specific lavatory in mind, use these general clearances for wall-hung, freestanding, and vanity-mounted units. The larger dimension is the preferred clearance, but if necessary, the smaller dimension can be used.

your plan is to start with the largest ones. If you know you want a whirlpool bath and separate dual shower, pencil them in first. (Hint: position the length of the tub perpendicular to the joists to distribute the weight safely.) To make the tub the focal point of the room, put it within a direct line of view from the door. If there will be a separate tub and shower, locate them near each other so that they can share plumbing lines. After placing the big items, locate your lavatory. Do you want two lavs or just one? Do you want two near each other or on opposite sides of the room? Do you want two toilets? Will two people use the room at once? Answer these questions before you pencil in the location. If you are placing two lavatories side by side, leave enough room for maneuvering space. One way to do this is to install storage between them, another is to install them at different heights.

Once the lavatories are in place, locate the toilet and bidet, if you have one. (A bidet resembles a toilet but is actually a basinlike device for personal hygiene.) The bidet is another item you will want to keep out of the sightline of the door.

With the main elements penciled in, start adding the extras—the windows, doors, sauna, and other amenities you are considering. Play with the design as much as you like, but remember to take practical matters like pipes and codes into consideration. Although there are recommended guidelines for comfort and convenience, only you will be able to determine what will be most comfortable for you. If you happen to be 7 feet tall, you can probably forget about the height clearances

smart tip PLANNING

The easiest and least costly remodels take advantage of the existing water supplies, drain lines, and vent stacks. If you want to add a bath or expand one, try locating it next to an existing one. Even stacking the rooms one over the other on different floors can take advantage of the existing lines and lower the cost of building or rebuilding the bath. Another cost-cutting measure is limiting the plumbing fixtures to two walls. This avoids the need for—and expense of—additional plumbing lines.

and raise them! Likewise, if you are a small person, lower the counters. Don't worry about being able to resell your home later; another person of your height may appreciate the comfort of a higher or lower surface. If the need arises, installing a new vanity with standard-height countertop is not easy, but it's not a major project either. It's far better to make the bathroom comfortable for you more than anything else.

bathroom types

The most-common-size American bathroom measures 60 x 84 inches or 60 x 96 inches. The most common complaint about it is the lack of space. The arrangement may have suited families 50 years ago, but times and habits have changed. If it's the only bathroom in the house, making it work better becomes even more important.

When planning the layout, try angling a sink or shower unit in a corner to free up some floor space. Also, consider installing a pocket door. Instead of a traditional door that takes up wall space when it is open, a pocket door slides into the wall. Another smart way to add function to a small bathroom is to install a pocket door into a wall between the toilet and the sink. That way two people can use the room comfortably at the same time.

You can also make a small bathroom feel roomier by bringing in natural light with a skylight or roof window or by replacing one small standard window with several small casement units that can be installed high on the wall to maintain privacy.

LEFT
It's the sophisticated mix of the subtle wall color and elegant materials that supplies the drama in this powder room. Wood floors in a medium tone complement the dark furniture-like wood vanity and black toilet. (Tip: Water and wood don't generally mix, so confine the use of wood floors to powder rooms only.) Note that the decorative hardware, mirror, lighting fixtures, and faucet all feature a similar metallic finish for a cohesive overall appearance.

ABOVE LEFT AND RIGHT
Shower dimensions vary widely from the minimum usable size to the most generous. When space is tight, consider a corner unit.
Don't forget to plan for clearance; the smaller dimension is the minimum clearance needed.

The Powder Room

The guest bath. The half bath. It has a lot of names, and it may be the most efficient room in the house, providing just what you need often in tight quarters. A powder room normally includes nothing more than a lavatory and a toilet. You can find small-scale fixtures specifically designed for it, from the tiniest lavs to unusually narrow toilets. In general, however, maintain a clearance that meets code on each side of the toilet and include comfortable reaching room for the toilet-paper dispenser. Most powder rooms measure at least 36 inches wide by 54 to 60 inches long, depending on the layout of the space.

Keep a small powder room as light and open as possible. Make sure the door swings out against a wall, or use a pocket door for easy access. If it must be accessible for someone in a wheelchair, include a minimum 5-foot-diameter circle of space in the center of the room, which is just large enough for turning around.

Because the powder room is often for guests and is normally located on the ground floor near the living area, take extra care to ensure privacy. The best location is in a hallway away from the living room, kitchen, and dining areas.

ABOVE
Unfortunately, this bathroom allows full view of the toilet from outside of the room.

ABOVE
Better privacy is obtained by flopping the toilet and the sink and reversing the door swing.

A Children's Bath

What should be included in a children's bath plan depends on the ages and number of children using it. If the bath will be for only one child, the design is easy. You can tailor it to him or her, taking care to plan for growing and changing needs. Anticipate the storage and lighting requirements of an older child's self-grooming habits, for example. However, if more than one child will use this bathroom, consider their genders and whether more than two will be using the bath at the same time. How many lavatories do you really need? The answer is at least two, if not more. The best designs for growing children include compartmentalized spaces—one for the toilet, one for the bath, and one for the lavatories. If this isn't feasible given the existing space, at least try to set the toilet apart. That way the children can take turns going to the bathroom and brushing their teeth for speedier bedtimes. Two special considerations in a kid's bath are territorial issues and

safety. Children are famous for protecting their space. Rather than fight this natural tendency, plan a cabinet drawer or wall shelf for each child. For safety, you may want to install countertops and sinks lower than standard height or build a step into the vanity cabinet's toekick area. Review other recommendations set forth in Chapter Three, "Functional Comfort," page 74. Lastly, remember what it was like to be a child. Get down to a kid's level, and design for a youngster's height and capabilities. Consult your children about decisions regarding the room's decoration.

The Family Bath

Compartmentalizing is the best way to start planning the family bath. But remember, when you separate the bathroom into smaller, distinct areas, you run the risk of making the room feel

LEFT
Crisp white ceramic tiles are highlighted simpy and effectively with a border of sharply contrasting red. The oval window and a scattering of decorative lighthouse-motif tiles add a touch of whimsy that works well in either a family or a child's bathroom.

OPPOSITE
Smart features for any family bath include a slip-resistant floor, towel hooks located within easy reach of the shower, and plenty of accessible storage.

cramped. Try to alleviate this with extra natural light, good arti-ficial lighting, and translucent partitions made of glass blocks or etched glass. Anything that divides with privacy while also allow-ing light to enter will help ease the closed-in feeling.

If separating the fixtures is not possible, include a sink in the dressing area within the master bedroom to provide a sec-ond place for grooming. Investigate building a back-to-back bath in lieu of one large shared room. Another popular option is to locate both the tub and the shower in the center of the room; install the bidet, toilet, and sink or sinks on either side in their own separate areas. To make the arrangement work, keep each side of the room accessible to the door.

BELOW, TOP RIGHT, AND BOTTOM RIGHT
When in doubt, stick to the classics. White cabinetry and chrome faucets and hardware—combined with beadboard and decorative moldings—add traditional appeal to a bathroom. If you choose white tiles, install them on the diagonal for texture and interest.

OPPOSITE
Stick to a monochromatic palette for materials if you aim to create a space that is serene but still great looking.

The Master Bath

The concept of the master bath has come of age. It is one of the most popular rooms to remodel and gives one of the highest returns on investment upon resale. It's where you can create that sought-after getaway—the home version of a European spa.

Some popular amenities to include in your plan are a sauna, greenhouse, exercise studio, fireplace, audio and video systems, faucets and sprayers with full massaging options, steam room, whirlpool tub, and dressing table. You are only limited by size and imagination—and some local codes.

Extras can be tempting but may require special planning. For example, you may need additional support in the floor, as well as supplemental heating and ventilation. You wouldn't want to slip in a tub and have it fall two floors to the middle of the living room. Unfortunately, this really does happen when the weight of an oversized contemporary tub is installed on top of a 50-year-old floor. Older houses simply weren't built to accommodate the volume of water some people now use when bathing.

Some of the best floor plans for the modern adult bath also include a separate room for the toilet and bidet, a detached tub and shower, and dual sinks on opposite sides of the room with adjacent dressing rooms and walk-in closets. Modern couples want to share a master bed and bath, but they also want to have privacy and the ease of getting ready in the morning without tripping over their mates. The only way to do this harmoniously is to mingle the parts of the room that invite sharing and separate those elements that are always private.

OPPOSITE BOTTOM LEFT
Though not large by today's standards, this bath offers many luxury amenities, including a spacious walk-in shower with both a fixed and a handheld showerhead and a convenient built-in toiletry niche.

BELOW
This deep tub is within easy reach of a warm, dry towel. Both the tub and the windows above it blend elements of modern and classic design.

RIGHT
A double-bowl vanity, outfitted with handsome hardware, features plenty of storage for two in drawers and behind doors.

design workbook
PLANNED FOR PAMPERING

calming colors

Surround a deep soaking tub with tile in colors borrowed from nature to create an earthy retreat. Complete the scene with dramatic lighting and greenery.

convenience

A niche that's lined with tile and built into one wall of the shower provides a handy spot for soaps and shampoos close at hand. (See also top left.)

practical amenities

Any shower can include multiple sprays, comfortable lighting, and a nonslip floor, far left. A handheld sprayer can be adjusted to different heights and is handy for cleaning the shower.

towel storage

A functional plan includes attention to all the small details, such as where you'll store the extra towels. (See also left.)

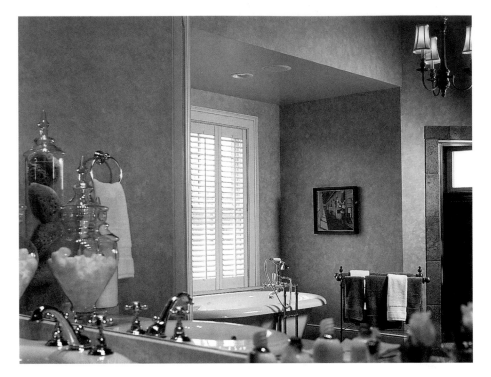

design workbook
TRADITIONAL MEETS FUNCTIONAL

sought-after features

The look is purely traditional, but the amenities are thoroughly modern and include a separate shower with a glass door and a deep soaking tub. Wood floors and base trim add grace.

beauty treatments

In an older home, where walls can be less than perfect, textured wallpaper, or one with a print, is an ideal way to hide blemishes while adding style. (See also top left.)

smart furnishings

Extra towels are kept at the ready on a freestanding rack with vintage flair. The furniture-like vanity and adjoining makeup table (left) offer storage for cosmetics and toiletries. A matching framed mirror, with built-in spotlights, spans the width of the vanity, making the room seem even more spacious.

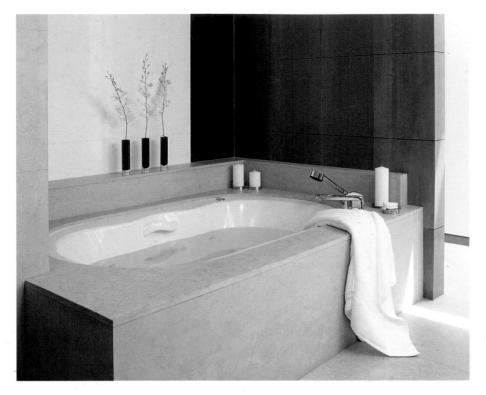

design workbook

THE ART OF CLEAN DESIGN

wood, naturally

Create a serene atmosphere by using natural wood that is properly treated. Here a mid-tone honey finish appears on the wood cabinetry and doors, as well as on the window, door, and base trim.

light, admittedly

Small casements admit light. Some of these units, and one in the shower, bottom far left, are ventilating.

concrete, simply

Concrete is an unassuming material, but it stands out in this modern bathroom. It provides the surface material for several walls, the floor, the vanity countertop, and the tub surround. (See also top left.)

space, openly

The glass walls and door of the shower enclosure, left, add the feeling of unencumbered space.

design workbook
MAKE ROOM FOR THE KIDS

keep 'em clean

Keep extra hand towels at the sink to encourage cleanliness. Baskets and towel rings offer stylish storage.

think safety

Provide a step-ladder until the littlest family members can safely reach the faucet handles. Install a faucet with stops that allow you to control the temperature of the hot water. (See also top right.)

use nonslip surfaces

A honed rather than a glossy mosaic floor tile, top left, will provide sure footing getting out of the bath.

pick colors wisely

Choose permanent elements, such as tile and fixtures, in classic colors that you can live with after the kids are grown. Save the fun colors for accessories. (See also left.)

design workbook
BATH SPACE DIVIDED FOR TWO

A heat register above the tub makes bathing cozy even on cool days. The window admits fresh air when weather permits, and a venting system combats moisture.

add convenience

Install a hand-held sprayer on the tub deck for rinsing hair and body. It's a convenience that also comes in handy for cleaning the large tub. (See also top left.)

soften edges

A softly angled countertop adds visual interest and allows more passing space for access to the separate, private shower room beyond. (See also far left.)

provide privacy

If there is space, locate the toilet in a private compartment, such as this one, left. If possible, add a window so the room doesn't feel like a closet.

design workbook
CREATE A PEACEFUL RETREAT

eliminate clutter

A vanity installed on legs expands the room visually. The unit also provides storage and elbow room for two to groom.

plan to relax

A soaking tub with a sloped back support, top left, coordinates with the room's stone and wood surfaces.

soak up the sun

The clear glass shower stall, bottom far left, allows natural light from the windows to spill into the room.

take it easy

Single-handle wall-mounted faucets keep the sink deck clear and easy to maintain. (See also upper left.)

please the eye

A stylish metallic storage cubby on wheels, left, mixes well with the natural materials and the room's aesthetic.

3

functional comfort

SAFETY FIRST   UNIVERSAL DESIGN   ACCESSIBLE DESIGN
ADAPTABLE DESIGN   DESIGN WORKBOOK

Wet floors. Bare feet. Electrical appliances in close proximity to water. These are some of the safety concerns to be considered
when designing a new bath. This is especially true when those using it
are the most vulnerable: children and the elderly. Slips, falls, and hot-
water scalds top the injury list. By the year 2020, more than half of the
population of the United States will be over 55 years old. Universal design
addresses the needs of that generation, as well as every other one. It is
design aimed at multigenerational households. As Baby Boomers bring
their aging parents home to live while still raising families of their own,

it is not uncommon to have small children and grand-

The bath as a
calming retreat
for mind and
body is today's
design mandate,
along with safety
for all who use it.

parents living under the same roof. Indeed, as our pop-

ulation ages in general, it behooves everyone to think

about design that is practical for everyone.

safety first

While form and function are two critical parts of any design, safety should reign as a primary factor in any bathroom remodel. Minimizing the risk of bodily injury only makes good sense. Take the following steps when designing for safety. And remember, you don't have to be very young or very old to be at risk of accidents, particularly in the bath.

smart steps
careful choices

Step 1 USE SLIP-RESISTANT FLOORING
Slips and falls are two of the top three on the injury hit list, so a good flooring choice is critical. Choose a slip-resistant surface such as textured tile or vinyl, or a matte-finish laminate flooring. If you decide on ceramic tile, be sure to purchase the type designed for flooring.

Step 2 INSTALL GRAB BARS
With the aging of society, grab bars are becoming standard accessories in bathrooms. If you don't need them now, you may in the future—even if it is only while you are recuperating from a sports injury or during the last few months of a pregnancy. Consider installing grab bars inside each tub and shower. You may even think about locating grab bars in the toilet area, particularly if there are people in your household who may have difficulty getting up and down.

   Many manufacturers offer grab bars in a variety of decorative styles and finishes. The good news is that they can also double as towel racks for added storage. But make sure walls are reinforced to receive the added stress of a person's weight before installing grab bars. Never use towel racks as substitutes for grab bars.

Step 3 REGULATE WATER TEMPERATURE
Regulating scalding temperatures in a tub or sink faucet is essential in any home, but especially when there are children or elderly persons using the bath. Install faucets with antiscald devices that prevent water temperatures from rising over 111 degrees Fahrenheit,

TOP
The more grout lines, the better the traction, so choose small tiles for the bathroom floor.

LEFT
This hands-free electronic-sensor faucet has a temperature-control lever that can be converted to a fixed setting.

OPPOSITE
When installing a sturdy grab bar on a tub or shower wall, be sure that it is firmly attached to the studs.

or opt for pressure-balanced valves that equalize hot and cold water. Consider a faucet that can be preprogrammed by you to a specific temperature. These controls should be childproof.

Besides opting for a faucet with a temperature regulator, you can prevent other related mishaps by installing tub and shower controls so that they are accessible from inside and outside the fixtures. The National Kitchen and Bath Association (NKBA) recommends locating shower controls between 38 and 48 inches above the floor and offset toward the room. Place tub controls between the tub rim and 33 inches above the floor, below the grab bar. Like shower controls, they should be installed offset toward the room. That way someone outside the tub or shower—or in a wheelchair—can regulate them.

Step 4 CHOOSE SHATTER-RESISTANT MATERIALS

Select tempered or laminated glass, plastic, or other shatterproof materials. Try to avoid any material or product that may break and present another hazard on top of a fall. This is particularly true in children's baths. Children tend to get rambunctious and exert more wear and tear on materials than a manufacturer may have anticipated. (Always choose durable, impact-resistant materials and fixtures in any child's room.) If you can, opt for a child-safe product over a luxury item if you can't afford both.

Step 5 DESIGN A SAFE SHOWER ENVIRONMENT

Besides shatterproof doors that open into the room (not into the shower) and temperature-control devices, there are other measures you can take to make showering pleasant and safe. For example, every shower unit should have a seat or bench that is 17 inches to 19 inches high and 15 inches deep, according to the NKBA. That way you won't put yourself at risk by standing on a soapy, slippery surface. Your back will thank you, too, when you don't strain it with deep bending at the waist to reach your feet.

Of course, you'll want a shower that is equipped with the latest In jetted sprayers and showerheads to make It look as glamorous as it functions, but keep the design simple. Avoid steps; install safety rails; and make the entrance wide enough to get in and out comfortably. Specify a 60-inch-wide entrance for a shower that measures 36 inches deep. For a compact 32-inch-deep shower, plan an entrance that is 42 inches wide.

Step 6 PLAN A SAFE TUB

It's not hard to feel like Cleopatra soaking in a luxurious sunk-in tub. And certainly a tub set into a sumptuous platform makes a big fashion statement. But the reality is that a tub that requires you to climb up or down steps can be hazardous. Steps can get wet and slippery, and you may lose your balance. When children will be bathing, supervision is a must. You may want to reconsider this design, especially if you will remain in the house as you age. What appears glamorous now could be impractical and dangerous when you're older.

Step 7 KEEP ELECTRICAL SWITCHES, PLUGS, AND LIGHTING FIXTURES AWAY FROM WATER SOURCES AND WET HANDS

Not only that, but make sure that every electrical receptacle Is grounded and protected with ground-fault circuit interrupters. These devices can cut the electrical current if there is a power surge or if moisture is present. Most building codes require installing them in kitchens, bathrooms, and any other rooms with plumbing.

Planning to include a light fixture above the tub or in the shower? For safety's sake, install it so that it is not within the reach of anyone—in either a sitting or standing position. Check local codes regarding this option.

Step 8 DON'T CLUTTER THE TRAFFIC AREA

If your bathroom is a compact 40 square feet, it can't accommodate an oversize tub or a bidet. Don't crowd in extra amenities and risk tripping over yourself or clogging walkways in the bathroom. There are minimum clearances you should adhere to for your own safety. An adjacent toilet/bidet installation, for example, requires a 16-inch minimum clearance to all obstructions. A water closet should be at least 3 feet wide by $15\frac{1}{2}$ feet long with a swing-out door.

Step 9 MAKE STORAGE ACCESSIBLE

If you can't reach a storage area without standing on the toilet, it's not useful. Ideally, storage for toiletries, linens, and the like should be no higher than 4 feet from the floor. Don't make it too low, either. You can avoid ill-advised bending by keeping storage at least 15 inches from the floor, says the NKBA. Locate storage for personal hygiene products within the reach of a person who is seated on a bidet or a toilet.

OPPOSITE LEFT
A shower door made of shatterproof glass or plastic that opens into the room is the only safe choice.

OPPOSITE RIGHT
Never keep soaps, shampoos, and other shower accessories on the floor. Install a shelf for them at a comfortable height.

LEFT
Extra towels within reach and good lighting keep this small space easy to use.

Step 10 INSTALL A SAFETY LOCK ON THE DOOR

For some reason the words "Do not lock the door" trigger an irresistible urge in children to do just the opposite. The best solution is to install a safety lock. This device, which is inexpensive, looks just like a standard doorknob with a little push-button lock on the inside of the bathroom and a pinhole in the knob on the outside. To release the lock from outside the door, insert an icepick or other thin tool into the hole and push out the button.

Lastly, use common sense. Some things should be obvious but are often overlooked. For example, people come in all sizes. Take an inventory of family members' heights to avoid placing sharp corners or racks at eye level. Children tend to grow, however, so this presents a challenge. The best approach is to place sharp-cornered items in spots that are away from any traffic patterns. For example, don't put a counter next to the tub where you will bump your hip every day as you step out of the bath.

Designing for safety is not difficult. All you need is a little thought and foresight. Run through the list of your family's functional needs for the bath, and then consider your physical safety. Is there a better way to arrange fixtures that will make it easier to maneuver? Does the design you have sketched out contain enough space for two people to use the bathroom at the same time? Answer these questions now, not after the fixtures have been installed.

universal design

By the year 2006, fully one-third of America will be disabled, chronically ill, or over the age of 65. Our society is aging, and our current housing stock is not designed to meet the changing capabilities of the aged. That is why the smartest trend in remodeling these days is universal design—an approach that opens the bath, indeed the entire home, to people of all different capabilities.

Universal-designed bathrooms are not the same as "accessible" ones. (See page 82.) They are simply more accommodating to people of all ages, sizes, skills, and capabilities. Begin by analyzing your lifestyle and your family's unique needs. Do you have someone in your house who must sit down while putting on makeup or shaving? Plan knee space under a sink or vanity. Does anyone have balance problems stepping into a tub? Install safety rails. Do you have small children who want to get ready for bed all by themselves without help from Mom? Perhaps a lower countertop and sink would encourage independence. Are you planning on having children in the future? What features would make your home more comfortable during pregnancy and your baby's infancy? Will you really be able to step into a sunk-in tub for a handheld shower during your ninth month? Maybe a separate tub and shower are more practical for the times you will be pregnant.

BELOW

Keep the space bright and well lit. Here, a glass-block wall creates a separation between the shower and tub without blocking light.

OPPOSITE

Accommodate everyone. This vanity has two sinks, but one has been elevated for a taller person's comfort.

Before incorporating every universal-design idea you can think of into your bath, decide how long you want to remain in the house. Statistics show that more often than not, today's homeowners stay put longer. If you plan on keeping your house into your golden years, include some accessible features. Good ideas include digital displays, which are easier to read; wider doorways to accommodate walkers, crutches, and wheelchairs; and minimum thresholds on interior and exterior doorways for easy maneuvering. The items specified in a universal design are usable by most people regardless of their level of ability or disability. For example, everyone can use lever door handles more easily than round ones, from people who have no hands to those whose hands are full. Universal design refers to products or to a more convenient placement of fixtures. Changing the counter heights in a bath may be more ergonomic for a couple whose heights are drastically different. The same would be true about placing a showerhead. Universal design addresses the scope of accessibility and attempts to make all elements and spaces usable by all people.

It may be worthwhile to look into some of the smart home technology—products that allow you to call your home from your cellular phone to turn on the lights, raise the thermostat, start running a bath, preprogram water level and temperature, and turn on the oven for dinner so that you have time for that long, hot soak. There are thousands of ways to make a home more usable. The key is to look at universal-designed products and match them to your house, your capabilities, and your anticipated future needs. Whatever you do, remember that universal design is supposed to make life easier. If adding these features will destroy your budget, don't add them. But remember safety—and keep the grab bars for days when you aren't so steady on your feet.

You may have heard the terms "accessible" and "adaptable" bandied about as though they are interchangeable with each other and with "universal design." In fact, they are different.

Accessible Design

Accessible design normally means that a home—or in this case a bathroom—is barrier-free. It also indicates that the room complies with the design guidelines for disabled people found in government regulations, such as the American National Standards Institute's A117.1 (ANSI A117.1-1986). There are a number of guidelines governing accessible design. Their goal is to provide criteria for designing for people who must use wheelchairs. Most accessible homes incorporate a number of fixed features that enable a disabled person to have easy access to areas such as the bathroom.

If there are disabled people in your family who will be using the new bathroom, you'll have to plan space accordingly, making sure there is adequate room for them to move around. You'll also need fixtures and fittings that allow people to care for themselves independently.

In addition to the safety features recommended earlier in this chapter, there are specific accessible-design guidelines, recommended by the NKBA, that you should follow. Begin by including enough space in your floor plan for a wheelchair-bound person to enter and maneuver around. Start with the entry. Doorways must be a minimum of 32 inches wide. Once inside, the person will need a passage that is at least 24 inches deep, moving into the room, and 36 inches wide. When you are sketching out the plan, include enough space for someone in a wheelchair to open or close the door. Because the amount of space depends on the type of door and the approach into the bathroom, you'll have to work it out with the disabled person in your home. Perhaps there is a similar entry into another room in the house where he or she can practice entering, closing, and opening the door while you take the measurements of the door swing.

OPPOSITE
If there's space, incorporate a place to sit while grooming at the vanity.

RIGHT
This toilet meets the criteria set by the American Disabilities Act (ADA) guidelines. The seat is 17 in. from the finished floor, in accordance with ADA standards.

With regard to fixture placement, the recommendations for clear floor space offered by the NKBA are listed in the box below. Just remember two things: First, it's okay to overlap clearances for different fixtures. Second, although you should always try to adhere to these professional guidelines, the available space may limit you. If you have to deviate a few inches here or there, the bathroom will still be the most accessible that you can make it. When you are ready to shop for fixtures and fittings, keep in mind you get what you pay for. As with products for standard bathrooms, there is an array (though more limited) that ranges from the purely practical to technological marvels.

In general, shop for a tub that allows a disabled person to transfer from a wheelchair to the bath with ease. There are tubs constructed with built-in seats that lift and rotate, allowing a person to slide on, rotate into the unit, and hydraulically lower himself flush with the bottom of the tub. This position is the most comfortable for bathing. A handheld sprayer will be handy, too, for warming up the water or rinsing hair.

Transfer showers permit a wheelchair-bound person to roll next to the unit, adjust the controls from the outside, and then back up and make a parallel transfer onto the shower seat using grab bars—or the wheelchair—as support. Standing individuals can use the shower by flipping the seat up or down, out of the way.

In the toilet area, you'll have choices, too. Instead of the standard 15-inch-high toilet, choose an 18-inch-high model, which makes getting up and down easier—even for people who are not disabled. Add a flush-handle extension, and install a toilet-paper holder with a controlled-flow feature. For accessibility, locate the holder 26 inches high on a wall in front of the toilet. A wall-mounted sink or one dropped into a countertop should be replaced at the universal-access height—32 inches. To accommodate someone in a wheelchair, plan a minimum 27-inch-deep-by-30-inch-wide knee space under the vanity or sink. Insulate any exposed undersink pipes to prevent burning. Lever faucets or touch-pad controls are recommended. If your budget permits, install touchless electronic faucets that sense motion. It's also practical to include a sprayer so that hair can be washed at the lav.

Adaptable Design

Adaptable designs are those that can be easily modified for use by a disabled person. They are normally used in multifamily rental housing so that the landlord can rent to a nondisabled person as well as a disabled one. The adaptable house incorporates some concealment of traditional accessible features. For example, an adaptable bath would have a door on the vanity underneath the sink that could be removed to make room for a wheelchair. There may be no steps at the tub and shower area—a good idea in every situation—or doorways may be extra wide.

OPPOSITE
The area below the sink in this vanity cabinet would have to be reconfigured to accommodate someone in a wheelchair.

smart tip ACCESSIBLE FIXTURE PLACEMENT

The table below shows the minimum floor clearances, in inches, recommended by the National Kitchen and Bath Association (NKBA) for placing fixtures in a bathroom that meets accessible design criteria. If you don't have enough floor space to meet them, at least use these minimum clearances as guidelines, but tailor them to your personal situation and available space as necessary.

FIXTURE	NKBA MINIMUM
Lavatory	30 x 48*
Toilet	48 x 48**
Bidet	48 x 48***
Bathtub	60 x 30****

In the case of a shower that is less than 60 inches wide, the minimum clearance should be 36 inches deep by the width of the shower plus 12 inches. A shower that is more than 60 inches wide requires 36 inches of clear floor space by the width of the shower.

* Up to 19 inches can extend under the lavatory.
** At least 16 inches must extend to each centerline of the toilet.
*** You may reduce it to 30 x 48 if space is tight, but that may compromise full use.
**** For a parallel approach. For a perpendicular approach, clearance should be 60 x 48.

design workbook

A BATHROOM FOR EVERYONE

barrier-free

This bathroom's large open plan can accommodate someone in a wheelchair. The drain in the floor is for the shower with an adjustable sprayer.

grab bars

Sturdy grab bars are important everywhere in an accessible bath, even above or next to the toilet. (See also top left, below left, and far left.)

within reach

On the shower wall, shampoo, soaps, sponges, and the like are kept at a lower height. Even the faucet handle is accessible. (See also left.)

easy transition

The space around the toilet is without barriers to make the transition from a walker or wheelchair easier. The grab bars provide the necessary support. (See also far left.)

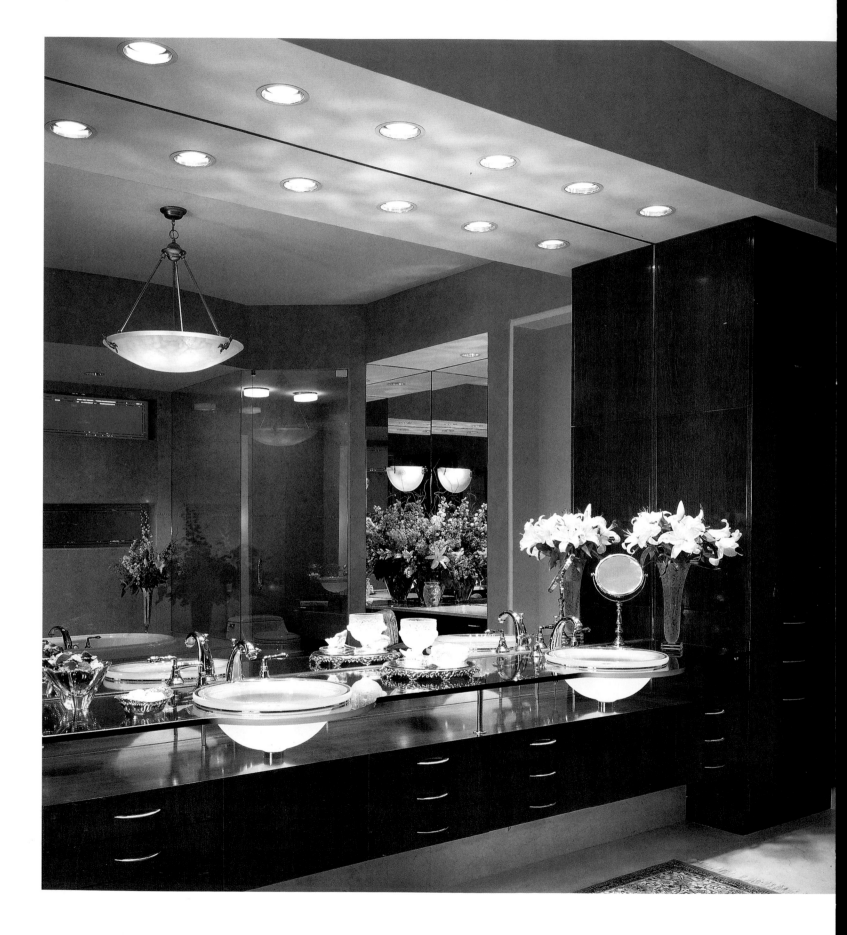

4

lighting your way

Bathrooms are the perfect place to play with light and its effects. There are so many elements that capture light, reflect it, and refract it. Good bathroom lighting brightens the space, makes it safe, and creates a pleasant, comfortable atmosphere. And, now that the bath has evolved into living space, the need for decorative lighting is more acute.

In this chapter, we'll explore the types of lighting and how you can use each one effectively to create a functional and unique lighting plan for your new bathroom. Learn how to maximize natural lighting and how to choose the right ambient, task, accent, and decorative lighting and more. We'll also discuss the types of bulbs; incandescent, fluorescent, halogen, and fiber optics. And, if you want to add dramatic effects to your new bathroom, there's advice for that, too.

Adequate, well-placed lighting is a necessity in the bathroom, where personal grooming tasks routinely take place.

Thankfully, modern technology has greatly enhanced glazing options with low-E glass to solve the problem of drafty, inefficient windows. Today it is possible to capture the daylight in your bathroom, as well as beautiful views, and incorporate them into your design without worrying about losing costly heat or air conditioning.

If privacy allows, a large window, a bay, or a bank of smaller units adjacent to the tub adds to the luxuriousness of the room. In a contemporary setting, install clean-lined casement windows. To blend with a traditional decor, consider an elegant arched window or a standard double-hung unit with muntins. If your bathroom will be adjacent to a patio, deck, hot tub, or private garden, think about including a pair of French or sliding doors in your plans.

Take a good look at the view you will be bringing indoors by adding a window or installing a set of glass doors that lead to the garden. Of course, not every house overlooks the ocean or snow-capped mountains, but even a pretty tree in the backyard and a few well positioned plants can make the view from indoors more pleasing. However, if your house is too close to the neighbors, a skylight, roof window, or glass blocks may be a better way to introduce natural light into the bath without compromising privacy or aesthetics.

No matter how much natural light you may have in the bathroom, there are times when you'll have to supplement it with artificial lighting. In fact, artificial lighting actually can enhance the effect of natural light at times.

natural light

The most natural light source and the best complement to your bathroom is daylight. Not only does the room look better when it's bathed with warm natural light, but it makes you look better, too. Imagine drenching yourself in light as you take your morning shower, or looking out at your garden while you soak in a tub of warm water.

ABOVE
When deciding on window size and placement, consider the view it will provide. The proximity and location of neighboring homes will determine whether you need some type of window treatment in order to maintain privacy.

OPPOSITE
Many homes now feature interior bathrooms or powder rooms with no available natural light. Good artificial light will make this type of space comfortable and safe to use.

the main types of artificial light

L ighting is the easiest way to set or change a mood. With one switch, your bathroom can go from a bright and busy grooming center to a softly lit, calm, and quiet getaway. If you've incorporated a variety of lighting options in other areas of the house but have neglected to do the same in your existing bathroom, now is a perfect opportunity. To do this properly, it's important to become familiar with the four main types of artificial light—ambient, task, accent, and decorative—and the options they present for your needs and comfort.

■ **Ambient Lighting.** Ambient, or general, lighting is illumination that fills an entire room. Simply put, it's standard general illumination. The source is normally from an overhead fixture, recessed lights, or even wall sconces, but the light itself does not appear to come from any one particular direction. Ambient light surrounds a room generally, not specifically. The most obvious example is fluorescent strips in the average office environment. A covering over the strips hides the source and diffuses the light throughout the room.

A wall sconce is another good example of ambient light. The fixture washes light up the wall for an overall glow. The wall reflects the light, which diminishes the appearance of a single source. While you can tell that light is coming from the sconce, the overall glow produced is diffused or softened.

The key to good ambient lighting is making it inconspicu-ous. It is merely the backdrop for the rest of the room, not the main feature. It changes with the surrounding environment— always providing light but never becoming obvious. For example, ambient lighting used during the day should blend in with the amount of natural light entering the room. At night, you should be able to adjust the light level inside of the home so that it doesn't contrast jarringly with the darkness outside.

■ **Task Lighting.** As the name implies, task lighting is pure-ly functional in purpose. It illuminates a specific area for a par-ticular job, such as putting in contact lenses, reading in the tub, shaving, or applying makeup. Task lighting is not meant to light an entire room.

LEFT
It's possible to find light fixtures that suit every style bathroom, from high tech to Victorian.

BELOW
A pair of sconces installed so that they are reflected in a mirror doubles the effect of the light available for grooming tasks.

OPPOSITE
If you like to unwind in the bath in the evening, be sure to install lighting over or near the tub.

Theatrical lighting around vanity mirrors is a great example of task lighting. It provides cross illumination and avoids shadows that overhead lighting often produces. Theatrical lighting can be too bright, however. Sconces on either side of a mirror produce light that is softer and more flattering.

Task lighting should always be included in a lighting plan for the bath, but its use should be optional. In other words, you can turn it on when you need it, and keep it off at other times. That's why task lights should not be on the same switch with a fixture that provides general illumination. The effect of having both on at once is bright and may be too harsh in your bathroom. It's also not the kind of lighting environment that is con-

ducive to grooming routines. To make it easy to see what you're doing, an individual fixture has to concentrate the light toward, but not directly on, a limited area.

BELOW
Sconces outfitted with dark shades direct illumination downward. The gold-tone finish inside the shades reflects a warm golden light that is appropriately dramatic in this powder room.

OPPOSITE
An offbeat yet artful fixture over a concrete vanity provides both general and task lighting in this contemporary bathroom.

■ **Accent Lighting.** Often the most forgotten in the bath but always the most dramatic, accent lighting draws attention to a particular element in the room, such as a handsome architectural feature or a work of art. You may ask, Why would I want to do that? The answer is simple, to create atmosphere. Accent lighting makes a room come alive. It creates a mood. It shapes space. For example, small uplights that are placed inconspicuously under a potted plant create an artful interplay of light and shadows on the wall and ceiling. Lights recessed into a soffit above a vanity cast a downward glow of illumination over a gorgeous countertop without spilling light into the rest of the room. Cove lighting installed above a tub delineates a bathing area dramatically.

Without accent lighting, there may be light but no focus, no character, no show business. With it, a design becomes exciting, theatrical, and rich.

■ **Decorative Lighting.** Where accent lighting draws attention to another object or surface, decorative lighting draws attention to itself. It can be kinetic, in the form of candles or a fireplace, or static, such as a fixed wall candelabra. Because it commands notice, it can attract or distract attention to or from something else. In this sense, it can be functional.

You can use decorative lighting in the bath to draw the eye upward toward a cathedral ceiling or to distract attention from the toilet and bidet, for example. By capturing your eye, decorative lighting forces your focus away from everything else. It doesn't highlight the way accent lighting does, and it doesn't provide a great deal of illumination as does ambient lighting. Decorative lighting is the device that most lighting designers love to use— the final stroke in a multilayered plan that combines more than one kind of lighting.

Some examples of decorative lighting include candles, chandeliers, neon sculptures or signs, a strip of miniature lights— any type of light that is deliberate and contrived. Include decorative lighting to unify a room—to strike a balance among all the types of lighting in the room, including natural light from the sun and moon.

the role of bulbs in design

Just changing the types of bulbs (or lamps as professional lighting designers call them) in your existing bathroom fixtures can make a major difference in the way the room looks, functions, and feels. Does this mean you should go out and replace all of your fluorescent lamps with halogen fixtures and call off the rest of your remodeling plans? That might be exaggerating the power of the right lighting design. But don't underestimate it, either.

OPPOSITE BOTTOM
In an all-white retro-style bathroom, industrial-inspired halogen fixtures with cobalt-blue glass shades illuminate adequately without creating harsh glare.

OPPOSITE TOP
Decorative incandescent crystal sconces and a chandelier not only focus the interest on the tub area, but provide task lighting for evening soaks, as well.

BELOW
In this tiny under-the-eaves powder room, a pair of jewel-like sconces focus the interest on the mirror and provide soft light that is complementary to skin tones.

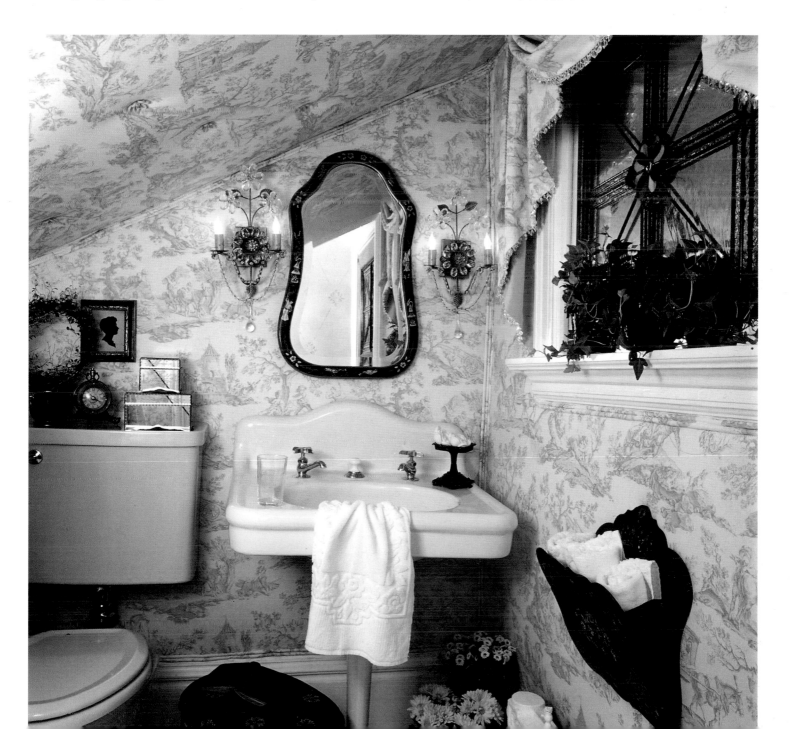

Understanding the differences in lamps will help you select the right light sources for every area in your bath. Light is like paint. You get different effects depending on the combinations of bulbs and fixtures that you use. And color is nothing but the reflection of different types of light. When selecting bulbs for your bath, always consider the important relationship that exists between color and light.

Standard Measurements for Color

Scales used universally in lighting assess the color temperature that the lamp gives off and how light from the lamp affects the objects it is lighting. The term color temperature describes the appearance of light in terms of the warmth or coolness of its color. Fluorescent lamps, which do not emit a continuous spectrum of light, are assigned a *correlated color temperature* (CCT) value. Lamp colors, which range in color from red to orange to yellow to blue to blue-white, are ranked according to the Kelvin (K) temperature scale. This will help you to select lamps and other lighting fixtures that are closely matched. You will also be able to vary the coolness or warmth of lighting for specific situations. Generally, light sources that are rated below 3,000K are considered warm, while those with ratings above 4,100K are perceived as cool. The recommended range for light sources falls between 3,000 and 3,500K.

Color rendition describes how a light source affects the perception of the color of an object that it illuminates. The Color Rendition Index (CRI) is a way of measuring a lamp's ability to render true color (the color of an object in sunlight). The color-rendering capabilities of lamps are rated from 1 to 100, with true color at 100.

RIGHT
The natural materials and finishes in this bath are enhanced by the warm glow of daylight pouring in through a pair of windows. Balance potentially dark corners in a room such as this by using warm, incandescent bulbs.

OPPOSITE BOTTOM
Because little grooming takes place in a powder room, the lighting can be more decorative than functional. Here a dark, translucent lampshade forces most of the warm light up and down in pools reflected on the wall.

Types of Bulbs

Most homes include a combination of warm and cool tones, so selecting bulbs that provide balanced lighting comfortably close to what appears normal to the eye is usually the most attractive choice. Experiment with various combinations of bulbs to create your own desired effect. This kind of layering and balance are two keys to a successful lighting plan. Here's a description of the most common types of bulbs and their advantages and disadvantages.

■ **Incandescent.** Like sunlight, incandescent bulbs emit "continuous-spectrum light," or light that contains every color. Illumination from these bulbs, in fact, is even warmer than sunlight, making its effect very appealing in a room. It makes our skin tones look good and even enhances our feeling of well-being. The drawbacks to incandescent bulbs are that they use a lot of electricity and produce a lot of heat. However, they come in a variety of shapes, sizes, and applications. (One type features a waterproof lens cover that makes it suitable for over a tub or inside of a shower.) These bulbs can be clear, diffuse, tinted, or colored, and they may have a reflective coating inside.

■ **Fluorescent.** These energy-efficient bulbs cast a diffuse, shadowless light that makes them great for general illumination. They are very energy efficient, but the old standard fluorescents are quite unflattering, making everything and everyone appear bluish and bland. Newer fluorescent bulbs, called triphospher fluorescent lamps, are warmer and render color in a way that more closely resembles sunlight. Fluorescents are available both in the familiar tube versions and in newer compact styles. Mixing these bulbs with incandescent lamps, plus adding as much natural light to the plan as possible, can make them much more appealing.

In some parts of the country, local codes require fluorescent lights to conform to energy conservation mandates.

■ **Halogen.** This is actually a type of incandescent lamp that operates at greater energy efficiency. It produces brighter, whiter light at a lower wattage. One disadvantage is a higher price tag. However, although halogens cost more up front, they last longer than conventional incandescents. Because a halogen bulb produces a higher heat output than other incandescents, it requires a special shielding. The low-voltage version of halogen bulbs produces a 50 percent brighter light than standard halogen bulbs. These are compact and use less electricity, which makes them more energy efficient, too. Low-voltage halogens are typically used for creative accent lighting in a room.

■ **Fiber Optics.** One of countless innovations gradually finding its way into the home, a fiber-optic system consists of one extremely bright lamp to transport light to one or more destinations through fiber-optic conduits. Used for accent lighting, fiber-optic lighting has the advantage of not generating excessive heat.

assessing your lighting needs

When a room is not bright enough, most people typically exchange low-watt light bulbs for high-watt versions. In a bathroom, with so many reflective surfaces, that may just create more glare. Wattage, in fact, is simply a measurement of how much electricity that a lamp consumes. The light output of a bulb is measured in lumens. So why do people always talk in terms of watts? Because the higher the wattage, the greater the lumens. When looking for the intensity produced by a lamp refer to it's candlepower (Cp). The more candela (units), the brighter the source.

LEFT
Compact spotlights add a modern look. They can be used for accent lighting, although their light can be decorative as well.

OPPOSITE LEFT
A rustic wrought-iron outdoor fixture looks at home in a bath with natural materials that include log walls and a slate floor.

OPPOSITE RIGHT
Frosted-glass shades diffuse the light produced by these sconces.

There are several important factors that will affect how much supplemental light you need. First, assess the reflectance levels in the room, or the amount of light that is reflected from a colored surface, such as tiles or a painted wall. Light colors are reflective; dark colors are absorbent. For example, white reflects 80 percent of the light in a room, while black reflects only 4 percent of it. In practical terms, a bathroom with a white vanity and tile and pale walls requires less light than one with dark cabinetry and tiles and dark walls.

Next, consider the size of the room. How high are the ceilings? High ceilings require brighter lights to dispel shadows. But you'll have to tone down the level of brightness in a room with low ceilings because light tends to bounce off low ceilings and walls. How many windows and skylights are there? Do they face the sunny south, or is their exposure to the north or somewhere in between?

There are no perfect stock formulas. But by looking at how each of these factors affects the others, you can make educated choices when developing your light plan. Keeping in mind the science and technology involved in lighting will help you assess your own requirements for the new bathroom. Ideally, you'll want to incorporate a variety of options for different activities, to create ambiance, and for decoration. Use the following steps to get started.

smart steps
do your homework

Step 1 EXAMINE YOUR ACTIVITIES
Above all, your lighting design should enhance the function of the new bathroom. Try taking out a splinter, bandaging a cut, or even cutting someone's hair without adequate lighting. Make a list of your daily routines in the bathroom, from morning to night. If you will have a laundry hamper in the bathroom, will you sort clothes there? Do you need specific task light for reading there?

Step 2 SKETCH AN INFORMAL PLAN
Refer to the base map you drew of the bathroom or make a new sketch. (See Chapter Two, "Making Space," beginning on page 42.) Circle the activity centers—the bath area, the sink, the dressing area, laundry center, and so forth. Everything you expect to do will require a different level of light. For example, do you need strong light to differentiate between blue and black socks? Of course, you'll want to light the tub area to make it bright enough for stepping in and out safely, but would you prefer a softer glow while you relax? A dimmer switch may be all you need.

Note each activity center with a G for general or ambient light, T for task light, A for accent light, and D for decorative light. In some places around the room, you may want to indicate more than one type of light.

You don't have to place decorative lighting into your plan unless it is a wired fixture, such as a neon sculpture or a track system of low-voltage halogens. But if you know you'll be using candles in the bathroom, it is a good idea to indicate them, too. That way you can specify an appropriate niche that will hold them safely where they can't tip over.

Designers typically determine light needs by using suggested foot-candle (Fc) levels for different activities and areas. Foot-candles, which refer to the amount of light that falls on a surface, are used primarily for directional lamps. To determine the foot-candle power you need to light an area, divide the candlepower (Cp) of the bulb by the distance (D) from the fixture to surface squared ($Fc = Cp \div D^2$).

Step 3 CHECK YOUR LOCAL CODE

Every municipality has its own codes regarding the placement of light and electricity around water. Before you purchase any light fixtures, check with the building inspector for the local code or speak with your contractor, who should be familiar with these issues. If you violate code, you won't pass inspection.

Step 4 VISIT LIGHTING SHOWROOMS

The best way to get ideas is to visit lighting showrooms and the lighting department in home centers. This will give you a chance to take an inventory of fixture types and styles currently on the market. Also, you can take advantage of the advice of lighting specialists employed at these stores. They can help you create the right plan and style of lighting for your bathroom. Bring along your sketch, your list of activities, as well as the design notebook you have compiled containing clippings, notes, sample plans, color charts, tile, paint, and fabric samples. The lighting designer can assess what you're after from there.

As you might already expect, some in-store advice is free. Ask about it. A few suggestions may be all you need to steer you in the right direction. Otherwise, you may want to consider an in-home consultation. Inquire about fees, which may be surprisingly affordable. Sometimes a modest investment in professional advice pays off handsomely in the final result—and in the discount that lighting designers can offer on the fixtures they sell.

Place your general lighting first, and then indicate where you'll need task lights. Start around the mirror. Plan lighting around the sides of the mirror for cross-illumination. This avoids the shadows that typically result from downlighting. Another tip: never focus a light to shine directly in the mirror or on a highly polished chrome faucet. The reflection of the bouncing light will distract your attention.

After you've noted every activity center for task lighting, decide where to install accent lighting. You might want some recessed fixtures over the tub. Maybe you can highlight beautiful crown molding or hand-painted tile. If you want to use accent lighting but don't know where it should go, ask yourself what is the most interesting feature in your bathroom. It may be something as simple as a framed print on the wall, a collection of pretty perfume bottles on the vanity, or a display on a small shelf.

There are also systems that computerize a variety of lighting options. A lighting specialist can design an entire program that sets the lights throughout the bathroom on a system devised for different moods and activities, such as showering, relaxing, exercising, washing the dog, or styling your hair. Everything is preprogrammed and controlled by one central panel. All you have to do is press the button corresponding to your selection. It definitely takes the guesswork out of layering light on your own. However, because of the sophisticated technology involved, these so-called "smart systems" can be high-priced, perhaps adding thousands of dollars to your budget.

decor and catch everyone's imagination. The past few years have proved to be a lighting designer's dream as fixtures have become more decorative and lighting schemes more varied and eclectic. From nostalgic reproductions to architecturally inspired designs and contemporary styles, there are models to suit any look in the form of wall sconces, chandeliers, strip lights, recessed canister lights, track lights, ceiling fixtures, and novelty types. The copious selection of finishes in all of these styles offers lots of excitement, too. Look for everything from colored, enamels to brass, chrome, pewter, nickel, and copper, which can be brushed, matted, or antiqued. There are also vintage designs in wrought iron and verdigris. For more interest, select fixtures with a combination of finishes, such as a verdigris with antiqued brass or copper. Mix matte and polished finishes. But stick to a style that is compatible with other elements in the room's decor.

finding the right fixture

Don't worry that you won't have enough options from which to choose in light fixtures. There's practically an endless number of styles on the market to match every

OPPOSITE
Lighting installed near the mirror helps to eliminate the shadows that form if you rely on overhead fixtures.

BELOW
These fixtures complement an innovative decor. Ask your lighting retailer about possible design assistance.

In a large room, combine more than one fixture type. In a bathroom, a ceiling fixture that includes a ventilating fan is especially practical. For accenting, pair uplighting fixtures, such as wall sconces, with downlighting types: recessed lights or a ceiling-mounted unit, for example. Install track lighting to wash an entire wall with illumination. Do this when you want to call attention to the architecture, a beautiful wallcovering, a special paint technique, or a mural. Experiment with light, using it to create different shapes, patterns, and textures on a plain wall.

Finally, before you purchase a light fixture, ask to see it lit up in the store. That way you can be sure it produces the effect you desire. It's also a good idea to show the store's lighting specialist your plans and perhaps tile, paint, and wallpaper samples so that he or she can guide you with your selection.

lighting a bathroom

In all but the tiniest of bathrooms, ceiling-mounted lamps are necessary for sufficient general illumination. A good choice is recessed lighting. How much you need, of course, depends on the size of the room. If it is less than 100 square feet, one fixture is sufficient. Add another fixture for each additional 50 square feet. If the surfaces around the room are light-absorbing dark hues, such as mahogany-stained cabinets, deep-colored walls, or black granite countertops, you may have to compensate with stronger lamps. If the bulbs you are using are not providing enough general light, you need to substitute them with ones that have more lumens. The next time you shop for bulbs, read the packaging, which indicates the lumens per watt (LPW) produced by a bulb.

Besides general illumination, recessed fixtures are ideal over a tub or shower area, or in a toilet compartment. Some are designed specifically for damp locations, and a variety of trim is available to create different lighting effects, such as wall washing and accent lighting.

LEFT
Combine several light sources and bulb types for interest and function. These illuminate the room as well as the contents of the cabinets.

OPPOSITE
This one-of-a-kind glass shade is an integral part of the vanity area's design.

Lighting for Glass and Mirrors

You'll need even, shadow-free lighting for applying makeup, shaving, or caring for hair. It should illuminate both sides of the face, under the chin, and the top of the head. Plan to use at least 120 incandescent watts. Never aim lighting into the mirror. Decorative sconces, installed face height, on either side of a small mirror do the job nicely. Place the fixtures no higher than 60 inches above the floor and at least 28 inches but not more than 60 inches apart, unless you pair them with another vanity light source. Ideally, combine side sconces with a fixture above the mirror.

If fluorescent side lights are mandated by your local code, you'll be happy to know that they come with a special coating that reduces glare and diffuses the light to minimize shadows. Install them up to 48 inches apart for sufficient lighting, and supplement them with recessed or surface-mounted ceiling fixtures. Also, use the deluxe warm white fluorescent bulbs that more closely resemble natural light. Make sure that the fluorescent fixture and lamps provide the best color rendering for makeup and realistic skin tone, within a range of 2,700K to 3,500K CCT. A large mirror, such as a three-way model used over a double vanity, will require a different approach: treat each lavatory as a separate area and light the vanity accordingly.

Depending on your design, you may want to install a series of side-light columns or span the entire mirrored wall with a fixture that integrates the entire sink/counter/mirror area. Mount the fixtures 78 inches off the floor for the best results, per the recommended guidelines of the American Lighting Association.

RIGHT
Fixtures installed on the mirror provide ambient and task light and add decorative interest to this traditionally styled bath.

Theatrical lighting strips are a great idea—if you install enough lamps. Too few very bright ones will create glare. Select units that use soft white lamps instead of clear globes or exposed bulbs. Because light is magnified by reflection in the mirror, cut glare by lowering the wattage; substitute 15-watt bulbs for ones that use 25 watts, for example.

Use a combination of side and overhead theatrical strips so that individual bulb wattage can be lower. Add a dimmer switch so that everyone in the house can adjust the light to his or her own needs. Recessed fixtures can be effective, especially incandescent fixtures with glass collars. Center them over the vanity countertop 36 to 48 inches apart.

Shower and Tub Lights

Light around the tub and shower area must be bright enough for safety and grooming. Recessed downlights or other fixtures designed for wet areas are fine. Shields eliminate glare, and shatter-resistant acrylic diffusers are safest. Any light fixture installed in a wet or damp area must be designed for such use, Your professional electrician will know how to handle the situation and can recommend the proper fixture.

LEFT
When selecting lighting for the shower, use only fixtures designed for installation in wet areas.

OPPOSITE
Frosted glass permits some natural light to enter but allows for privacy. Small recessed fixtures overhead illuminate the tub.

smart tip LIGHTING EFFECTS

Be creative when thinking about architectural lighting. Install it along the top or bottom of cabinets or inside the cove of a raised ceiling. Integrate a lighted valance with a vaulted ceiling or a curtain sweep, install a small spotlight in a wall niche, or highlight molding. For the best result, analyze the room's potential for using architectural lighting effectively before making any decisions or changes. Ask yourself:

■ Is the reflected wall or ceiling surface sufficiently attractive to call attention to it?

■ Can I alter the look of the lighting by tinting the color of the surface upon which it reflects?

■ Can I increase lighting efficiency by painting the interior of the valance, cove, or soffit white? (Remember, light-colored surfaces are reflective.)

■ Does the reflected light enhance the rest of the room's lighting scheme?

■ Is the ceiling high enough (at least 8 feet) to keep the light from spilling onto the walls? (The top of the cove should be at least 18 inches from the ceiling.)

design workbook
VARY THE LIGHT TO SUIT NEEDS

combine forces

In all but the smallest baths, provide varied sources of light and fixture types to ensure function, comfort, and safety.

light the way

The proper number and placement of recessed light fixtures can provide a suitable amount of overall illumination. (See also top left.)

illuminate task areas

In addition to the vanity mirror, a magnifying mirror with a built-in lamp will make applying makeup or shaving easier. (See also far left.)

bring in natural light

A shower that is enclosed almost entirely in glass is bright and cheerful in the morning and admits additional natural light into the rest of the bathroom. (See also left.)

5

ventilation & heating

MOVING AIR   WARM COMFORT   DESIGN WORKBOOK

No room will produce more water vapor than the bathroom. Opening a window isn't always the most pleasant or economical way to vent the room, either. Besides minor annoyances like foggy mirrors and chilly floor tiles, how much attention you pay to venting and heating the room affects larger, more important issues: your health and comfort, as well as the prevention of moisture damage to the new bathroom itself. A bathroom vent should be able to exchange the entire volume of air from the room in 30 minutes. The best place to install the vent is near the ceiling, to ensure that warm moist air is adequately vented. Ductwork can be routed through an outside wall or through—but not into—the attic. If moisture lingers after you've dried off and are ready to leave the bathroom, a fan with a timer switch is the answer.

Sufficient ventilation and heating will keep your bathroom comfortable and create a fresher, healthier environment.

If the main heating system doesn't adequately warm the bathroom, there are things you can do to give it a boost. A portable oil- or water-filled baseboard heater is one solution. Another helpful device is the toe-kick heater, which can be installed into the toe space under a vanity cabinet. Whatever you do, make sure it is safe and permissible by local codes.

BELOW
Opening a door and windows will bring fresh air into this room, but a venting system is necessary for expelling airborne moisture.

OPPOSITE
Double-glazed windows are better insulated against heat loss, so you can install large ones like these without sacrificing comfort.

moving air

Adequate ventilation is a must in any humid environment, and you can't get much more humid than the modern bathroom retreat. Those fabulous home-spa features (multiple showerheads, rain bars, jetted tubs, and saunas) use more water than standard fixtures, raising the humidity level in the bathroom accordingly. The only solution is a good ventilation system.

Ventilation combats the steam and condensation that cause mildew, rot, and deterioration of the bathroom's surfaces and the surrounding rooms or exterior walls of the house. If you haven't installed a proper moisture barrier between the bathroom and the exterior wall, you may face serious structural damage in addition to peeling and chipping paint.

If you install glossy ceramic tiles on bathroom surfaces, your ventilation needs are greater than if you use an absorbent material, such as cork. (Unfortunately, many absorbent materials aren't appropriate for the bath because they can decay and spread bacteria.) Even glossy paints can resist absorption and create problems with mildew and mold.

OPPOSITE

Here, a heater has been installed in the toe-kick area (under the vanity). This thoughtful device keeps feet warm on chilly mornings when stone or ceramic tiles can be especially cold.

ABOVE

This master bath has been designed to incorporate the outdoors into the room. Operable windows and a glass door can assist in venting the room of stuffy air and damaging moisture.

Beyond concerns for bathroom surfaces and structural elements, imagine the air quality in a stuffy, unventilated bathroom. Noxious fumes released into the air by cleaning solutions and grooming products, including hair spray and nail polish, pose a health risk. The most common side effects of this indoor air pollution include eye, nose, and throat irritation. Not exactly the picture you had in mind when you dreamed of creating a relaxing, sybaritic haven in your new bathroom.

Turn the page to find what you can do to ensure a fresh, healthy environment in the new bath.

smart steps
clear the air

■ **Step 1** INCORPORATE A WINDOW INTO YOUR DESIGN

The simplest form of ventilation is natural: a window. If you don't have access to a window (for example, the bathroom is not located on an outside wall), investigate a vented skylight or a roof window. Many come with electrically operated controls for easy handling. In a multilevel house, you can even install a shaft or tunnel that makes it possible to bring light and air from an operable skylight or roof window into a bathroom on the ground floor. Some of these units work by remote control for easy operation.

After you choose your windows and decide where they will work best, you may need additional measures to control glare, reduce winter heat loss, block unwanted summer heat, and create privacy—all while preserving the view outside. This calls for flexible controls that respond to the time of day, season, and outside weather.

Window accessories take many forms: storm windows of glass or plastic that you add to the inside or outside of the window; awnings or shutters mounted on the outside; or pleated shades, blinds, and curtains mounted on the inside. Most window treatments can be adjusted, seasonally or daily.

Choose a window control system that will both enhance your comfort while in the bathroom and help create the design expression that you are seeking. You can take your first cue from the climate. Window treatments for a hot climate should block direct sunlight. In a cool climate, use insulated window treatments to block drafts. Next consider privacy. If your bath window is vulnerable from the yard or neighboring house, choose a device that can be easily closed to block all views to the interior. Your final selection will have to accommodate the type and size of windows, the appearance you want, and your budget. Here are a few of your choices.

BELOW
A roof window like this one installed over the shower area boosts natural light and can be opened for ventilation.

■ **Storm Windows.** If you live in a location with cold winters and are beginning with old leaky windows, you can either replace the windows with newer, more energy efficient windows or tighten them by caulking and weather-stripping and adding a storm window to the inside or outside. Just make sure that the storm window can be opened and closed without removing the entire unit, particularly if it is located above the ground floor.

■ **Blinds.** Adjustable blinds are a good way to control light glare and create privacy, though they don't add to the window's energy efficiency. Two types of slatted blinds enable you to direct the sunlight where you want while maintaining a view to the outdoors. Horizontal blinds made of aluminum or vinyl slats are the best for south-facing windows because they can shut out the higher amount of sunlight that comes from the south. They also ensure privacy. You can angle them upward to let light in but prevent the view into the bathroom, or close them tight to completely block the light when it is too hot.

For windows on the east and west, vertical blinds work the best by blocking out the low-angle sun that adds so much heat on summer afternoons. Available in various tints, fabrics, and widths, vertical blinds can be rotated to direct sunlight where you want it. They can be closed completely or drawn open to the side of the window.

■ **Shades.** Unlike blinds that contain slats to block out light when fully closed, some shades let in light even when closed. You can, however purchase sun-blocking shades, but they are higher priced. In addition to standard roll-up shades, there are pleated and accordion styles, as well as Roman shades. In this moist room, make sure any fabric is treated for mildew resistance. Pleated shades stack rather than roll up, and ride down in tracks. Single-layer pleated shades fold like an accordion. Another type is made of two layers of fabric and forms a honey-comb shape when viewed from the side.

■ **Curtains.** Curtains control outdoor glare and create privacy. But like fabric shades, bathroom curtains should be treated to mildewcide. At least, they should be washable. You can purchase insulated curtains, but they are not washable. It's better to combine a bathroom curtain that you can throw into the washing machine with an insulated shade or blind.

■ **Awnings and Shutters.** Awnings can block direct sunlight from entering the window. They work best on south-facing openings, though. To keep late afternoon sunlight out of west-facing windows, you'll need awnings that lower to cover almost the full depth of the window. Shutter your bath windows only if you want to fit the other windows on the house similarly; otherwise your bathroom windows will look out of place. For privacy, you may want to consider interior wood shutters instead of fabric window treatments. You can easily mount them to an entire window unit or the bottom half of a double- or single-hung window.

smart tip HEATING AND WINDOWS

If you have ever sat in a tub below a poorly insulated window on a January night, you know how unpleasant it can be to feel a steady stream of cold air wafting down on you. A well-designed window will inhibit heat loss in winter, as well as heat gain in summer. So, if you don't plan to exchange an old unit for something new and more efficient, think some more. Between 20 and 30 percent of a home's heat loss is through old windows. Today's windows are better sealed against leakage and better insulated against heat loss through the glass. If you can't enjoy that new soaking tub year-round, is it worth it?

Wherever you live, for a more comfortable and even temperature in your new bath, consider replacing a less-efficient window with one that is double-glazed (thermopane) and is protected with low-emissivity (low-E) coating on the glass. For easy maintenance and operation, choose a unit clad in aluminum or vinyl. Don't forget: an insulated window treatment can save energy, too.

■ Step 2 INSTALL A VENTILATION SYSTEM

In most jurisdictions, local building codes require fans in bathrooms that do not have windows. Even if you have access to natural ventilation, there are certain times you won't want to keep a window open (the middle of winter, for example). There are three types of bathroom ventilation systems available for your consideration.

■ **A Recirculating Fan.** As its name implies, a recirculating fan simply moves the air around in the room. It does not vent air to the outdoors, but it does help to dispel some of the moisture that has accumulated on surfaces during bathing. It is not the most effective option, but it is an inexpensive one because it doesn't involve ductwork. If ductwork is too expensive for your budget, consider installing a recirculating fan.

■ **A Ducted System.** A ducted ventilation system discharges humidity in the bathroom by removing moist, stale air and odors and venting them through ductwork to the outdoors. If the unit is properly sealed, it will not bring outside air indoors. It simply clears the room of bad air and allows fresh air from the rest of the house to circulate into the bathroom.

Sometimes, these fans are vented into the attic. This is not recommended because of the potential for causing moisture damage under the attic eaves.

Some of the latest options offered by manufacturers of bathroom fans include remote-location units, built-in lighting, units that include heaters, multiple speeds, quiet operation, and an automatic-on feature that is triggered by a device that senses high levels of humidity.

smart tip FANS

Especially in large bathrooms, more than one fan is recommended for efficient venting. Of course, first check with your local building department about codes that may stipulate where to install bathroom fans. If possible, include a fan in the toilet area, one near the shower, and one over the bathtub.

■ **Room Exhaust Fans.** Separate exhaust fans mount anywhere on a ceiling or outer wall of a new bathroom. The main thing is to connect the fan to the outside via a vent cap on the roof or sidewall. To match the fan capacity to the room size, divide the volume of the room by 7.5. For example, if you are adding a new bathroom measuring 7 by 9 feet with an 8-foot ceiling, its volume is 504 cubic feet. The proper-size fan will have a capacity of 504 divided by 7.5, or 67.2 cubic feet per minute (cfm). Exhaust fans vary between 75 to 600 cfm, so the smallest one would suffice. Noise is another issue when shopping for exhaust fans. Fan noise is rated in sones. The quietest bath exhaust fans come in at around 1 sone—about the level of a refrigerator fan. Fans can be rated as high as 4 sones.

warm comfort

Something that is often neglected in design is sufficient heating. This often happens when a room is added on to accommodate another bath. The capacity of the current heating system may not be adequate to serve the new space efficiently. For your own comfort, therefore, check the heat-load capacity of your system. Your local utility company may be able to assist you in this matter, or call in a heating specialist for professional advice.

Unless you're adding on a lot of extra space to the house, you won't have to replace your heating system (although if it is old and burns a lot of energy, this may be a good time to replace it with a more efficient model). Often you can supplement the existing system with alternative sources of heat. Some of your choices include:

■ **Radiant Floor Heat.** Energy-efficient, invisible, and space-saving (no radiators or baseboard heaters) radiant heating is a trend that is growing in popularity. The system uses hot water or electric wire coils installed underneath the floor. As the floor warms up, heat rises to take the chill out of the rest of the room. This may be a viable option if you are replacing a floor or building from scratch. However, some flooring types may be incompatible with this type of heat. Good candidates include ceramic tile, slate, and wood.

■ **Towel Warmers.** Imagine wrapping yourself in a toasty towel to ease the transition from steamy shower to cool room. In the past, this is the kind of "luxury" item you may have associated with a first-class hotel, but towel warmers are becoming more standard fare in residential design, particularly in master suites. There are two types: traditional hydronic radiator-compatible models and those that work on electricity and simply plug into a wall socket.

■ **Toe-Space Heaters.** Another amenity growing in popularity—especially in master baths and children's bathrooms—toe-space heaters fit neatly into dead space under a vanity cabinet. They provide a pleasant blast of warm air on demand. Just flip the switch to turn cold tile floors toasty. Although electric heat sources can be expensive compared with other types, these devices aren't meant for constant use. In the long run, they shouldn't add too much to your energy bills.

■ **Heat Lamps.** Using infrared bulbs that radiate heat into the space, heat lamps are usually mounted in the ceiling around the tub or outside the shower area. In most cases, they are monitored by a timer.

■ **Convection Heaters.** A convection heater warms the air, then circulates it using a small fan that is built into the unit. For an easy convection heat source, install an electric heater on the bathroom wall or ceiling. Many models also come with exhaust fans and lights to combine ventilation and heating. Other forms of convection heat sources include gas heaters, which are available for propane or natural gas, and heat pumps. If you choose a gas heater, always properly vent it to the exterior of the house.

LEFT
Heated towel warmers like these may seem like a luxury, but they can also help to warm the room. These units are wall mounted and hard-wired electric. Other electric types may be freestanding and plug into an outlet. Another type, hydronic, is heated by hot water from a home's hot-water system.

design workbook
CREATE A HEALTHY ENVIRONMENT

heat in

Glass block for exterior walls is insulated for energy efficiency, so it's suitable near the tub. (See also left.)

moisture out

A ventilating fan is a must in a bathroom. Some models operate quietly, too. (See also left center.)

lose the cold feet

Stone tile is beautiful but cold underfoot. The solution is to install a heater in the area under the vanity.

a light idea

Some fans are combination units with light fixtures, bottom left, that come in several decorative styles.

suit yourself

If it becomes too warm while you're grooming, you can close the registers in the toe-kick area. (See also far left.)

6

fixtures & surfaces

PRODUCT HYPE   FIXTURES AND FITTINGS   STORAGE
SURFACING MATERIALS   PRODUCT SHOPPING LIST   DESIGN WORKBOOK

The latest trends in bath design call for glamorous materials and fixtures. Today's top designers are combining glass, stone, ceramic, metal, and wood and adding luxurious amenities for a sophisticated look. The products that you select to outfit your new bathroom will affect both your design and your budget. If you choose top-of-the-line products, expect a top-of-the-line bill. Factors that influence the cost of new fixtures, cabinetry, countertops, and flooring include updated technology and type of finish. The smarter the device, the more you'll pay for it. Likewise, the fancier the finish, the higher the price tag. But cost does not always reflect quality, nor does it equate necessarily with satisfaction. And quality and personal satisfaction are the most important factors to consider when making any product selection.

Exquisite products and finishes have elevated the status of building and plumbing materials for the bathroom.

So, how can you make smart choices about items like tubs and showers, tile, faucets, sinks, and cabinets? How can you tell whether a product is reliable and will endure the daily abuse of water and moisture? Are there basic differences that make one faucet or a particular toilet better and more efficient than another? How can you ensure that you'll be satisfied in the long run? To find out, you can do a little research. Shop around. Visit bath designer showrooms, read books, and don't be afraid to ask questions. Otherwise, you can take your chances. If you're not the gambling type, however, the information here will help you to select products and materials for your new bath with confidence.

product hype

A high price does not always mean high quality. Find out what is different about a toilet that costs $100, for example, and one that sells for $300 or even $1,000. This way you can decide whether the higher price is worth it. A knowledgeable salesperson will be able to tell you. If not, contact the manufacturer. Many have toll-free numbers and Web sites set up to handle consumer questions. Sometimes the price hike is because of a feature you can't see. For example, a faucet with replaceable parts costs much more than a new faucet with parts that cannot be replaced. Follow these steps when you're evaluating possible purchases for your bath.

smart steps
shop wisely

Step 1 WEIGH YOUR OPTIONS

Analyze the benefits and the risks that come with each product. Once you have that information, a decision will be easier. If you are sprucing up an old bath or adding a new one in a house that you expect to sell soon, you might install a less-expensive countertop material, for example. But if you are making a major investment, you might be happier in the long run with something that may cost more but gives you greater satisfaction and will be more reliable for years to come.

Step 2 SEEK RELIABLE ADVICE

Ask the manufacturer about the expected life of the product and its efficiency.

Don't take advice from a store clerk unless he or she is an experienced remodeling professional. Talk to your contractor, who may be familiar with the product or can pass along critical feedback from other clients who may have purchased the same item or something similar to it.

LEFT
A gorgeous custom-made tub that has been sculpted in granite stands like a massive work of art in a bathroom that is almost austere in every other aspect.

OPPOSITE
Classic in style, a pedestal lav always adds a grace note to a bathroom. This reproduction style strikes a pretty pose in front of a modest, painted bead-board wainscot.

Step 3 DON'T MAKE A CHOICE BASED ON STYLE OR COLOR

It doesn't work for cars, and it won't work for building materials. Sure, style and color are important, but it's just as easy to find a first-rate faucet that looks great in your new bathroom as it is to find one that looks fabulous but performs poorly. Opt for quality.

Step 4 BE WARY OF SOME HANDMADE PRODUCTS FOR THE BATH

You may be tempted by a handsome unglazed sink from a chic pottery shop. Certainly, it will add a unique cachet to your design, but an unglazed sink may not meet local code. Don't buy on impulse before checking out the building codes in your area. If there's any doubt in your mind, ask if you can leave a refundable deposit on the item, and then speak with your contractor, who should be familiar with the rules.

Step 5 PRORATE COSTS

You may be dismayed by the initial sticker price, but when you divide the cost of the product or material by its anticipated longevity (how many years you expect it to last), you may be amazed at how reasonable it really is. Of course, this won't alleviate an immediate cash-flow problem, but it will ease some of the sticker shock. An expensive product that will last for 20 years may be a better choice than a cheaper one that may have to be replaced in five years. Again, weigh that decision against how long you plan to stay in the house. Are the extra benefits worth it?

Step 6 INQUIRE ABOUT GUARANTEES AND SERVICE OPTIONS

Some offers are definitely better than others. Look at the warranties that come from the manufacturer, as well as those offered by the place of purchase. A store may offer immediate replacement of the entire unit. While this may sound great, it isn't if you have to pay for labor or schedule time off from work for the removal and reinstallation of a fixture. Find out whether there is a better way. If all that is wrong with a faucet is a faulty washer, you may not want to yank out the entire unit. It should be your call. Find a place that offers a warranty based on the problems with the product. And always get written copies of all warranties from the store or your contractor.

Step 7 DO A REALITY CHECK

Look at your situation, and choose the best products and materials for the way you live. Don't get swept away by bells and whistles that can blow your budget. Your bottom line isn't bottomless, so compare each extra-cost feature with your real needs and lifestyle. A sumptuous shower with 18 massaging hydrojets may be your fantasy, but if your morning routine is a race against the clock to get to work on time, invest the extra money elsewhere. Besides, multiple shower outlets, as well as large tubs, may require larger water-supply lines, and that might not be an option.

Step 8 LEAVE NOTHING TO CHANCE

Investigate every option and every detail for the new bathroom. Don't find yourself bemoaning what you should have done when it's too late. After you sign the final check is not the time to realize that you could have installed an in-line heater to keep bath water consistently warm or a steam unit in the shower. Discover everything that's out there—before getting started. Don't miss any of the fun stuff, and you won't have any regrets or extra charges for changes made after work has begun. Read magazines and check manufacturers' Web sites for new product introductions.

Although the trend in recent years has been to increase the size of the bathroom, most are still relatively small compared with other rooms in the house. Yet this room remains the most expensive per square foot to renovate. This behooves you to invest wisely.

fixtures and fittings

Thirty years ago, items like tubs, toilets, and sinks were standard fare, not to mention boring. Who could have imagined they would generate the excitement they do today? As bathrooms have been enlarged and elevated to symbolize status in American homes over the last couple of decades, second only in prestige to kitchens, even the most pragmatic items have become elements of design. But in addition to appearance, the workings of bathroom fixtures have become technologically more glamorous, as well.

Tubs

Soakers, whirlpools, classic claw-footed models, tubs for two, spas for four, contoured shapes, ovals, squares, or rounded tubs, streamlined or sculptured models, tubs with neck rests and arm rests; tubs in a variety of colors; freestanding tubs; tubs set into platforms; tubs that you step down into: it's your soak, so have it your way.

Ask yourself: How do I like to bathe? Do I prefer a long, lingering soak or an invigorating hydromassage? A popular trend is the sunk-in whirlpool tub, which comes with an array of therapeutic and relaxing options in the form of neck jets, back jets, side jets, multiple jets, or single jets that are installed in the walls behind the tub. Custom designs in solid stone, concrete, and metal are emerging at the high end of the market. But tubs are usually made of one of the three following materials:

■ **Fiberglass.** Lightweight and moldable, a fiberglass tub is the least expensive type you can buy. But it's prone to scratching and wear after about a dozen years. Some come with an acrylic finish, which holds up against wear longer.

■ **Solid Acrylic.** A mid-price-range product, acrylic is more durable than fiberglass and less prone to scratching because the color is solid all the way through. Whirlpool tubs are usually made of acrylic because it can be shaped easily. It's also lightweight, an important feature for large tubs that can put stress on structural elements under the floor.

■ **Cast Iron.** An enamel-coated cast-iron tub will endure as long as your house stands. It's a heavyweight, though, and not recommended for a large soaking tub.

The most common size for a tub that backs up against a wall is 32 x 60 inches, but you can find models in widths of 24 to 42 inches. If someone in the family is tall, no problem: you can purchase a standard tub that's up to 72 inches long.

OPPOSITE
A bathtub with a nostalgic "French telephone" faucet features a practical hand sprayer.

BELOW
A colored concrete surround and deck accommodates this white porcelain tub. Modern-style faucet handles enhance the sleek look.

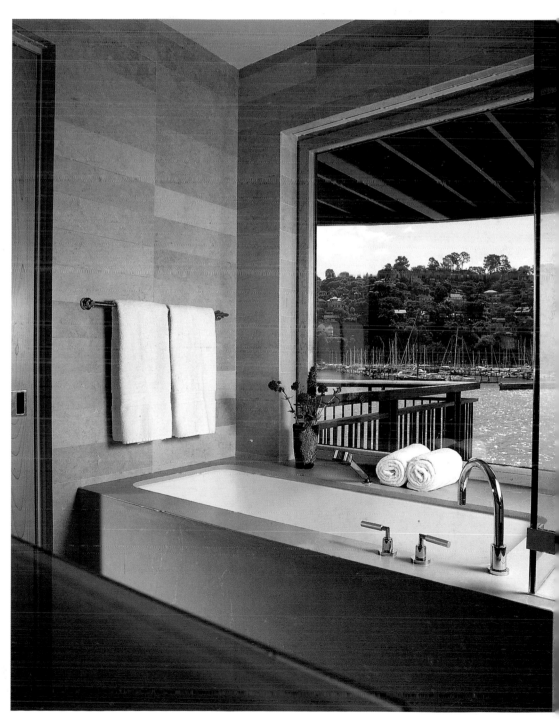

Showers

Spectacular spray options and spa features make showering as sybaritic as the most luxuriously appointed bath. Shower units separate from bathtubs can be prefabricated from molded fiber-glass or acrylic. They come in widths of 32, 36, and 48 inches, with a standard depth of 36 inches and a height of 73 inches. Custom-built showers are typically constructed of solid surfacing, ceramic tile, or stone. Top-of-the-line features include massaging hydrotherapy sprays, steam units, a foot whirlpool, built-in seat-ing and storage, even a CD player. Amazing technology lets you enjoy a full body massage on a miserly amount of water. Although by law new showerheads may not deliver more than 2.5 gallons of water per minute, you can install as many as you wish.

The only things limiting your shower are your imagination and your budget. If you want it, it's out there. Unless you're inter-ested in a strictly no-frills unit, think about installing more than one showerhead and mixing and matching devices from any or all of the following three basic spray categories.

■ **Fixed Spray.** This type is mounted on the wall or ceiling, and it may or may not come with a massage option. New ver-sions include a device that propels water into the air to give you a hydromassage. Other nifty models, called rain bars, let you close your eyes and pretend you're in a rain forest where gentle mists pamper you with a soft rinse. Or you can opt for a cascade of water that is delivered by a waterfall spout.

■ **Handheld Spray.** A handheld device is convenient for directing water where you want it. It stores in a wall-mounted slide bar and can be adjusted up and down to accommodate the tallest or shortest bather. Combine a handheld spray with a stationary showerhead, and then add a massager with as many as eight settings and a body brush, and you've created a cus-tom shower environment that rivals any first-class away-from-home spa.

■ **Jet Sprays.** Just like those used in whirlpool tubs, shower jet sprays are housed behind the shower walls. One manufacturer

offers as many as 16 with its shower unit. Jet sprays can be pro-grammed to various settings. Get a therapeutic hydromassage to relax stiff neck muscles or a sore back, for example. If you like, select a full body massage at whatever intensity is comfortable for you.

Toilets

Believe it or not, you do have choices when selecting a toilet for your new bathroom. Vitreous china is still the material of prefer-ence, but there's a wide range of colors and style options to suit contemporary or traditional tastes. If you like something sleek, select a European-inspired elongated bowl. Though toilet sizes vary somewhat among manufacturers, an elongated bowl will extend about 2 inches more into the room than a standard ver-sion. The typical height of a toilet seat is 15 inches, but some come as high as 18 inches, which can be more comfortable for tall or older persons.

Another option is whether your new toilet will be a one-piece, low-profile model or a two-piece unit. There are style vari-ations within both types, including rounded bowls, long square shapes, and vintage looks. Nostalgia lovers will be happy to know that Victorian-style high-tank toilets are still manufactured. Scaled-down toilets are available, too, for condos and apart-ments that are short on space or for tiny powder rooms, such as those tucked into a stairwell.

ABOVE RIGHT
You can install one or more tile-size water sprays, like this one, in the wall or combine them with other sprayers in a large shower.

OPPOSITE
The manufacturer of this suite of fixtures was inspired by the elliptical soaking pools, and the boulders surrounding them, in natural spas around the world.

If you are still fighting in your household about whether the seat should be kept up or down, give peace a chance. Look into these new gender-friendly features: a lid that automatically lowers when the toilet is flushed or the toilet that shines a red light in the bowl when the seat is up and a green light when the lid is down.

If that isn't enough, consider a residential urinal. One type fits into the wall like a built-in laundry hamper; another sits on the floor next to the toilet.

Besides style and type, you should be concerned about the flushing mechanism. Although appearance factors can affect cost (low-profile, one-piece, and elongated bowls being at least twice the price of standard two-piece models), the flushing mechanism may have an even bigger impact on the price tag. New toilets must conform to the government's low-flush standard, which mandates that no more than 1.6 gallons of water be used per flush. (Older models used a whopping 5 gallons or more per flush.) There have been complaints about the effec-

tiveness of low-flush toilets, but the technology is improving.

There are three basic types of flushing mechanisms, listed in order of their cost, starting with the least expensive.

■ **Gravity-fed** is the standard device used by two-piece toilets. Press down the lever, and the force of the water that is released from the tank and into the bowl flushes waste down the drain and out through the pipes.

■ **Pressure-assisted** uses water pressure in the line to compress air in a chamber in the toilet tank. Flushing releases the air, forcing water into the trap.

■ **Vacuum-flush** makes use of two internal chambers to create a vacuum that is released when you flush. The result forces water into the bowl and through the trap.

If you have any qualms about purchasing one of these new toilets, talk to your plumber. This person has first-hand knowledge regarding models that are efficient and effective. Don't just shop for looks or depend on a manufacturer just because you know the name.

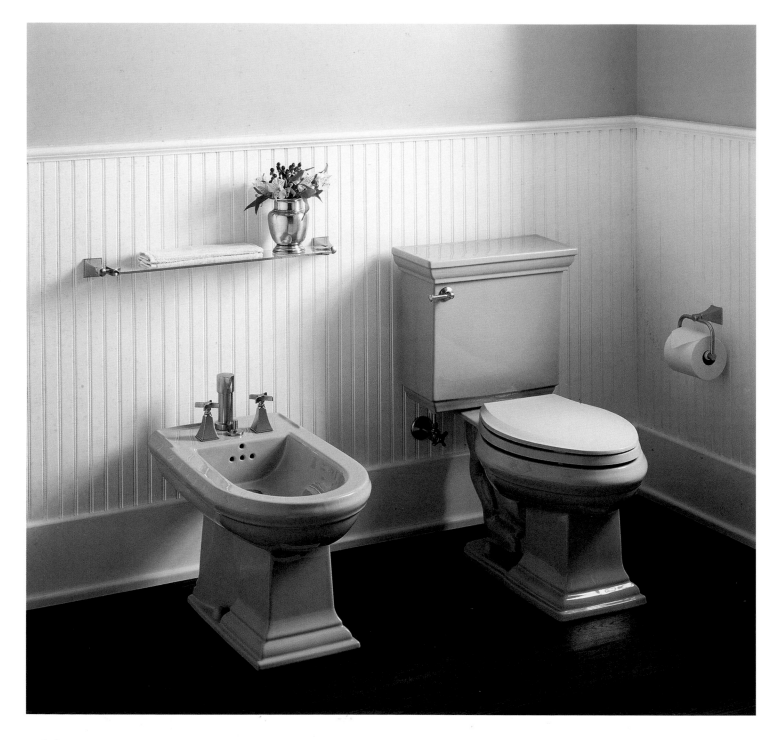

Bidets

A standard fixture in European bathrooms for decades, bidets have been slow to catch on in the American market. They are gaining in popularity, however, particularly in new construction and high-end remodeling where they are becoming status symbols in master suites. Typically a bidet is selected to match the toilet, and the fixtures are installed side by side.

Lavatories

You may find it practically impossible to select one lavatory over another because they come in so many sizes, shapes, styles, and colors. Sensuous curves, sculpted bowls, and beautiful, durable finishes can make this vessel a work of art—and an important element in your overall design. Today's lav can be made of vitreous china, cast iron, enameled steel, fiberglass, acrylic (solid-surfacing material), stone, faux stone, or metal. Its finish may be hand painted, contoured, beveled, brushed, or polished. A sink can be a freestanding pedestal or it can be mounted to the wall or be part of a vanity top.

Vanity sinks, in pairs or as a single lav, are designed to be installed in one of four ways:

■ **Self-Rimming.** The bowl of a self-rimming sink is surface-mounted: you drop it into the counter, and the ridge forms a seal with the countertop surface. This ridge or rim can be decoratively carved or handpainted.

■ **Under-Mounted.** If you want a tailored look, an under-mounted sink may be for you. In this instance, the bowl is attached underneath the countertop for a clean, uncluttered appearance.

■ **Integral.** As the word "integral" implies, the sink and countertop are fabricated from the same material—stone, faux stone, or solid-surfacing. The look is sleek, seamless, and sculptural.

■ **Rimmed.** Unlike a self-rimming sink, a rimmed model requires a metal strip to form the seal between the top of the sink and the countertop.

There are attractive, shapely lavs in every price range. Colored lavatories are usually a bit pricier, as are delicate hand-painted designs. If you will do anything at the sink besides washing your hands and face and brushing your teeth, consider choices in design and size carefully before you buy.

Something that is too shallow, for example, may not be practical for rinsing hair or hand washables. A pedestal sink may be pretty, but if you apply makeup, style your hair, or shave, this type may not provide surface storage for related grooming items. Think before acting.

OPPOSITE
A toilet and matching bidet feature architectural design details that blend in with similar motifs in a traditional-style home.

BELOW
An above-counter, or vessel-style, lav is an artful element in a powder room or a master bath. This one has been installed atop an antique dresser that has been retrofitted to house plumbing.

LEFT
Ultra modern and chic, this European-style lever faucet has an elegant satin nickel finish. It has a raised spout that is high enough above the lav to deliver water without splashing.

OPPOSITE
This updated version of a cast-iron Victorian tub is deep for soaking. It rests above the floor on wooden legs and features a convenient integrated chrome towel bar.

Inquire about the faucet's valving, too. Many faucets come with a washerless ceramic or nylon cartridge that lasts longer and is less prone to leaks. Ceramic is the better choice. Select finishes depending on your taste and other elements in the room that you may wish to coordinate with the fittings. Finishes include chrome, polished brass, enamel-coated colors, pewter, nickel, gold, and gold-plated.

Make a fashion statement by mixing finishes or selecting a design with inlaid stones or gems. You have a variety of options from which to choose, so take advantage. Think of faucets as jewelry for your bathroom, and accessorize accordingly. There are three basic types of faucets for your consideration:

■ **Center-set faucets** have two separate valves (one for hot, another for cold) and a spout that are connected in one unit.

■ **Widespread faucets** feature a spout with separate hot- and cold-water valves. All appear to be completely separate pieces.

■ **Single-lever sets** have a spout and a single lever in one piece for one-hand control.

Whatever your decorating motif, you can find faucets to coordinate with the look you wish to achieve. Reproduction styles in brushed-metal finishes look good in traditional decors, as do graceful gooseneck spouts. Sleek geometrical shapes with enameled or high-gloss finishes enhance contemporary designs. While you're admiring faucet styles, remember function. Cross handles are charming, but they can be difficult to grasp for the elderly, disabled persons, or the very young. Levers and wrist blades make more sense in these cases.

Faucets and Other Fittings

Like showers, faucets are no longer just conduits of water. Today's faucet technology gives you much more control over your water. You can program an instrument for a pulsating effect or select the gentler rhythm of a babbling brook or a cascading waterfall; preset water temperature; enjoy a hot bath that never gets cold; protect children from scalding.

For quality, inquire about the materials used for the faucet's innards. The best choices are solid brass or a brass-base metal, which are corrosion-resistant. Avoid plastic—it won't hold up.

Grab Bars and Towel Bars

The first thing to remember is that grab bars and towel bars are not interchangeable items. A grab bar must be installed so that it securely attaches to wall studs or blocking behind a shower or bathtub or at the toilet. For quality, shop for grab bars made of solid brass. For style, coordinate them with other hardware, such as the towel bars, faucets, and cabinet pulls and handles.

storage

Undoubtedly, an important aspect of your new bath's design is storage. You'll probably need plenty of it, too. Besides toiletries, grooming aids, extra linens, a hamper, and cleaning supplies, you may want to store gym equipment, books, magazines, and CDs, particularly if the room will be a place you can go for adult quiet time after a day at work or with the kids.

No matter what the size of the bathroom is, it should contain a reasonable amount of storage. To get it, you'll have to thoroughly analyze the space and prioritize what items you must have handy, as well as any extras you'd like. Believe it or not,

even a tiny 5- x 7-foot bathroom can accommodate spare rolls of toilet paper, additional bars of soap, a blow dryer, and curling iron, as well as a stack of clean towels, as long as you think storage issues through at the design stage of the project.

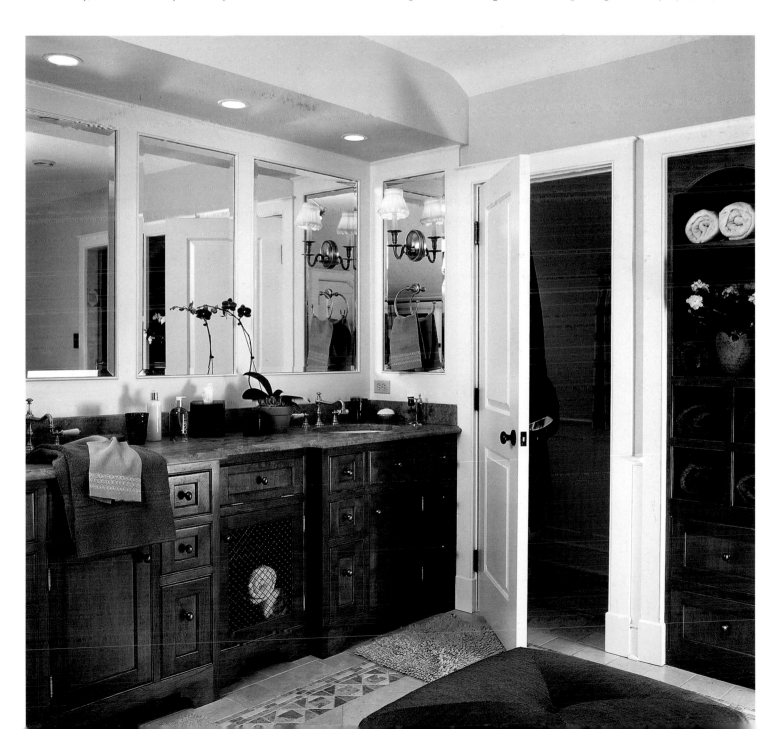

If you are working with a professional, he or she will have more than a few storage tricks to offer if you are specific about what you need. Is a vanity sufficient? Will it be for one or two people? Do you require a medicine cabinet? How about a linen closet? Extra shelves? Drawers?

When you are acting on your own, go back to Chapter Two, "Function: Up Close and Personal," and review the questions about how you intend to use the new bath. Make a list of everything you want at hand. Scale back if necessary, but start big. For example, if your children will bathe in this room, include storage for bath toys—ideally, someplace other than along the ledge of the tub. If you'll shave, groom your hair, or apply makeup at the vanity, pencil in a place—not the countertop—to keep essentials away from the sink and protected against exposure to water or dampness. If you're tired of toting dirty clothes downstairs to the basement or ground-floor laundry room, see whether your plan can accommodate a compact washer/dryer. These are just a few of the storage-related issues that could affect your project.

In any event, it's likely that you'll want at least a vanity and a medicine cabinet in your new bath. Like fixtures and fittings, they make important statements about how the new space will look, as well as how it will function.

Vanities

Today there are many creative ways to approach the vanity. One is to treat the vanity as a decorative receptacle for a drop-in sink with just a countertop and legs and no attached cabinetry. If you can sacrifice the storage a cabinet provides, this option will add drama to your design, especially if the countertop is outfitted with handsome tile, stone, or colored concrete. But if you're limited by space and have to make the most of every inch, a vanity cabinet is the wisest choice. Cabinets are available in three ways:

■ **Stock.** Factory-made in a range of standard heights, sizes, and finishes, stock vanities are usually, but not always, the most economical type. Styles are limited.

smart tip STORAGE

A linen closet inside the bathroom is an amenity some homeowners think they can't afford if the space is small. If that's your dilemma, a little rethinking and reshuffling may yield the necessary room you thought you didn't have. First, reconsider the size of the bathroom fixtures you've been planning for your design. Would a smaller tub, shower unit, or vanity relieve the crunch? Second, think about building the closet into an adjoining room, if possible. Your designer may have other ideas, too.

You can't go wrong if you make good use of even the smallest pocket of space, like the toe-kick area at the bottom of the vanity, where you can install extra drawers or a slide-out step for kids who can't reach the sink yet. If there's a low-profile toilet next to the vanity, extend the countertop over the toilet. Ask your builder to suspend a drawer from underneath the extension. Don't forget to include a built-in shelf inside the shower or tub enclosure to hold soaps and shampoos. Use the wall space; install open shelves for extra towels, bars of soap, bubble bath, and the like. Better yet, think about opening up a wall between two studs and using the dead space for recessed shelving. One caution: just don't cut the studs in case it is a load-bearing wall.

■ **Semi-Custom.** Factory-made and outfitted with custom options upon your order—and usually midrange in price—semi-custom vanities include extras such as pullout bins, spin-out trays, special door styles, or custom finishes.

■ **Custom.** Built-to-order to your bathroom's specifications, custom vanity cabinets can be designed by your architect, interior designer, or designer/builder. This is typically, but not always, the most expensive option.

OPPOSITE

A vanity can take on the appearance of a freestanding piece of furniture. This one is custom made, but a dresser could easily be repurposed with a sink and a countertop.

BELOW

This semi-custom cabinet has been custom-finished to match the floor and tile in the shower. On the inside, special compartments have been created to organize small items.

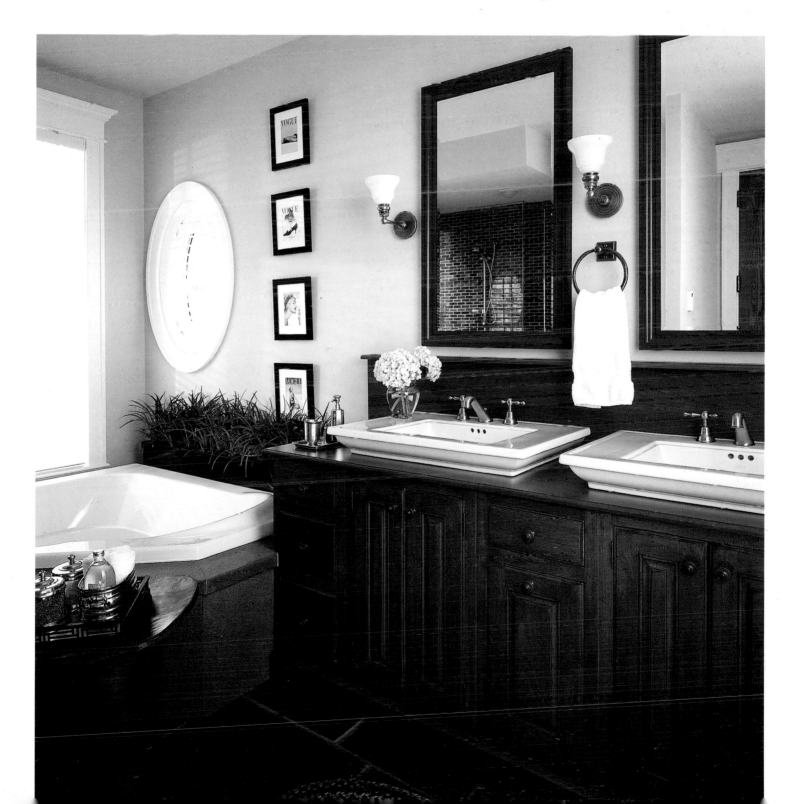

A popular vanity trend is to retrofit a piece of fine wood furniture, such as an antique chest, with a lav, reproduction fittings, and an elegant countertop. But the wood surface has to be sealed with a protective coating that resists water and mildew. If you don't have the right piece of old furniture but want the same look, check out the new cabinet styles offered by manufacturers today. Look at designs created for the kitchen as well as the bath. Some are interchangeable and display furniture details. Fluted pilasters, elegant moldings, and filigree patterns adorn many models that also come with beautiful hardware and finishes engineered to hold up to humidity and mildew. They wipe clean easily, too, so you don't have to worry about upkeep.

Whether you select a vanity style that is traditional or contemporary, with a plastic laminate, metal, or wood finish, give the vanity cabinet as much consideration as you would if it were meant for the kitchen. Top-of-the-line solid-wood construction may be too expensive for most budgets. However, a sturdy plywood frame combined with dovetail and mortise-and-tenon joinery is excellent, too. Make sure the interiors are well finished, however, and shelves aren't flimsy.

There are basically two construction styles for stock and semi-custom cabinetry: framed and frameless. Both are available from American manufacturers.

■ **Framed.** Framed cabinets feature a full frame across the face of the unit. Hinges may or may not be visible.

■ **Frameless.** Frameless cabinets, often called European-style cabinets, are built without a face frame and therefore have a sleek appearance. Because the doors are mounted on the face of the box or are set into it, hinges are typically hidden inside.

Medicine Cabinets

You can find attractive medicine cabinets that can be wall-mounted or recessed into a nonload-bearing wall between the studs. From ultra contemporary visions in glass and lights to designs that make bold architectural statements, there's a wide selection of stock units to match any decor or cabinet style.

When shopping for a medicine cabinet, look for one that offers room for everything from toothbrushes to shaving cream and bandages. Choose one that spans the width of your vanity

LEFT
This pair of medicine cabinets is deceptive because they appear to be shallow. Actually, the cabinet interiors, which are recessed into the wall, are deep enough to hold bulky rolls of toilet tissue.

OPPOSITE
A countertop made of slate tiles has a rustic appeal. Each tile has its own natural texture and color, which makes the surface uniquely handsome.

or beyond it, if wall space allows. In other words, buy the largest one you can find! Look for deep shelves that accommodate objects larger than a small pill bottle. Built-in lighting, swing-out mirrors, and three-way mirrored doors are some of the other extras you may want in a medicine cabinet. In addition, some units come with a lock or a separate compartment that can be locked to keep potentially dangerous substances out of the hands of young children.

surfacing materials

Even in well-ventilated bathrooms, steam and moisture can take their toll. So it's important to select materials for the walls, floor, and countertop that can hold up to water. Plastic laminate and vinyl are good choices that come in different price ranges, depending on quality. Generally they are the most affordable. Ceramic tile, solid-surfacing materials, and concrete fall into the middle to high end of the spec-

trum. Installation and finishing techniques affect their costs. Natural stone, such as slate, granite, and marble, are at the high end of the price scale.

Laminate

Consider affordable laminate for your bathroom countertops and flooring. When installed on counters, plastic laminate resists moisture superbly and is easy to maintain. It comes in so many colors, patterns, and textures that finding one to coordinate with other elements in your design—fixtures, tile, wallcovering—is easy. Want a countertop made of slate or marble, but can't afford the real thing? Does a buttery leather, smooth suede, cool glass, or warm wood appeal to you? A faux version in laminate may be the answer. Besides giving you a price break, plastic laminate offers a practical alternative to some natural materials that would be too delicate for such an installation. In that sense, it is versatile and practical. Plastic laminate countertop material comes in various grades. At the very top of the line is "color-through" laminate. As opposed to laminate with color on the surface only, this type will not show a brown seam line at the edge because color is solid all the way through.

With regard to flooring, the latest laminate products boast easy care, as well as moisture and stain resistance. Manufacturers now offer literally dozens of designs that are dead ringers for real wood or stone. These come in either tongue-and-groove planks or as tiles. Like sheet laminate used for counter tops, laminate flooring is more economical than the natural materials it portrays, and in most cases it installs right over old flooring.

Vinyl

Textured vinyl flooring is an excellent choice for a bathroom designed for children or elderly people because it is the most slip-resistant material you can install. (If it isn't textured, however, it can be slippery when wet.) You don't have to sacrifice style for safety, either. Manufacturers have developed an extensive array of colors, patterns, and textures from which to choose. Unless you buy the highest grade, vinyl is the least expensive flooring on the market. Keep in mind, though, that inexpensive vinyl products tend to crack and tear even under normal use, and the finish wears off easily. For durability, you'll have to pay for a higher quality.

Ceramic Tile

Besides its practical features, including imperviousness to water, durability, and easy maintenance, ceramic tile offers the greatest opportunity to bring style and personality to your bathroom. Use it to add color, pattern, and texture to the wall, floor, or countertop. Enclose a tub or shower with it. Tile is versatile. It comes in a variety of shapes, sizes, and finishes. Use decorative tiles with hand-painted finishes or raised-relief designs to create a mural or mosaic. You're only limited by your imagination. Hand-painted tile is expensive, but it allows you to do something truly unique. If cost is a factor, accent standard tiles with a few hand-painted designs. Or achieve a similar look at less cost by using mass-produced tiles with silk-screened designs. Visit a tile showroom in your area or the design department of a nearby home center to get ideas. Mix and match embossed tiles, accent and trim strips, edges, and a contrasting colored grout (the compound that fills the joints). For long-lasting wear and easy maintenance, always apply a grout sealer in areas exposed to water, such as the countertop or tub surround.

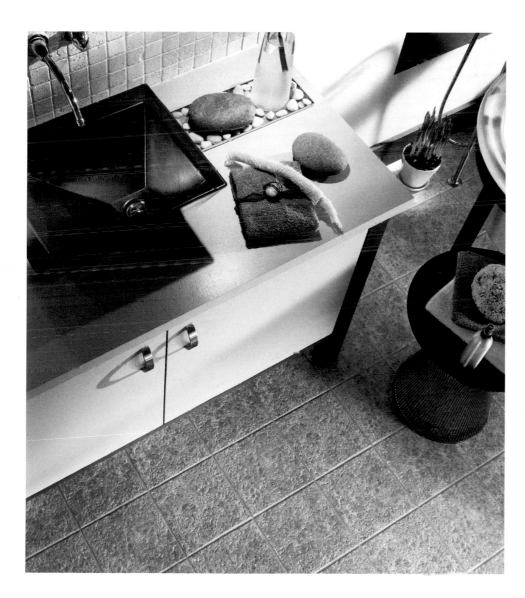

OPPOSITE
Ceramic tile is a classic surfacing material for the bath. Here, matching floor and wall tiles open up the space.

LEFT
This textured resilient sheet vinyl floor realistically mimics the look of stone tile, and it's slip-resistant.

Consider the finish when you're shopping for tile. There are two kinds: glazed and unglazed. Unglazed tiles are not sealed and always come in a matte finish. If you want to use them in the bathroom, you will have to apply a sealant. Glazed tiles are coated with a sealant that makes them impervious to water. This glaze can be matte finished or one that is highly polished. Highly glazed tile, however, can be a hazard on the floor. Instead, opt for a soft-glazed tile intended for floor installation. When shopping, inquire about the manufacturer's slip-resistance rating for the tile you are considering. It's also a good idea to make sure any tile selected for a countertop installation can handle the spills and knocks that occur typically around the sink and on the countertop surface.

Solid-Surfacing Material

An extremely durable, easily maintained synthetic made of polyester or acrylic, solid-surfacing material is used to fabricate countertops, sinks, shower enclosures, and floors. It's not cheap, costing almost as much per linear foot as granite or marble, but it wears long and well. It is impervious to water, and any dents or abrasions that may occur over time are repaired easily with a light sanding. Solid surfacing now comes in a variety of colors and faux-stone finishes.

Stone and Concrete

Granite, marble, and slate are probably the most expensive materials you can choose for a floor or countertop. They are all extremely durable and rich looking. Two other stone materials, limestone and concrete, are finding their way into the creative hands of designers today, too. Unlike granite, marble, and slate, limestone has more of a primitive, textured appeal. Concrete offers flexibility. It can be colored, shaped, carved, and inlaid with objects like pieces of tile for a sophisticated effect. Concrete offers lots of new creative possibilities, but it cracks easily.

When considering any one of these options for flooring, however, remember that they are cold underfoot and unforgiving—anything you drop that is delicate will break. Stone may pose a safety hazard on the floor, too, because it gets slick when wet. A fall on a stone floor can cause serious injury. Older persons and children are at particular risk. If you choose one of these materials, use slip-resistant carpeting over it.

As countertop material, any one of these materials introduces a dramatic element to the room. The only thing you have to worry about is sealing your natural countertop properly against moisture.

These materials are also heavy, so beware if you plan to use them on a floor or to fabricate a tub or shower. Check with your builder or a structural engineer to find out whether you'll need additional support under the floor to carry the extra weight.

Wood

Wood has typically been taboo in the bathroom because of its susceptibility to water damage, mildew, and warping. However, if you seal it properly with one of today's sophisticated high-tech finishes, you can use it safely. This should come as good news to homeowners who like the incomparable warmth offered by real wood. On the floor, walls, or countertop, wood requires a urethane finish. Some kinds of wood, such as teak, hold up better than other softer, porous types like pine.

OPPOSITE
Wood can pose problems in a bathroom. But here, a teak floor adds warmth and comfort to the Asian-inspired design that emphasizes natural materials.

ABOVE
Painted wood paneling in the tub area has been treated to withstand moisture. Still, it will need maintenance over time.

product shopping list

I t's a good idea to keep a record of what products you are buying for the new bath; each one's style name or number, size, color, and quantity; the manufacturer's name; and the cost. To make that task simple, here's a list of the typical purchases involved in a new bath. You can use the list to do your shopping and to keep records.

Description	Style	Size	Color	Qty.	Mfr.	Total Price
PERMANENT FIXTURES						
Bidet						
Door						
Pedestal lavatory						
Shower door (if separate)						
Shower stall						
Standard tub						
Toilet						
Vanity lavatory						
Whirlpool tub						
Window						
FITTINGS						
Grab bars						
Handheld sprayers						
Lavatory faucet set						
Shower curtain rod						
Soap dish						
Standard towel bars						
Shower faucet set						
Toilet paper holder						
Toothbrush holder						
Tub faucet set						

Description	Style	Size	Color	Qty.	Mfr.	Total Price
STORAGE						
Cabinets						
Medicine cabinet						
Open shelves						
Vanity						
SURFACING PRODUCTS						
Countertop						
Floor tile						
Other flooring						
Paint						
Wall tile						
Paneling						
Wainscot						
Wallpaper						
LIGHTING and ELECTRICAL						
Ceiling fixtures						
Exhaust fan						
Exhaust fan with light						
Fluorescent strips						
Heat lamp						
Heated towel bars						
Mini light strip						
Mini spotlights						
Miscellaneous						
Recessed canisters						
Track lights						
Wall sconces						

design workbook

IN THE VERY BEST TRADITION

seamless renovation

Traditional-style fixtures and finishes are just right for this new master bath created from a small room.

bathing beauty

A pretty pedestal tub, deep enough for a full-body soak, fits neatly inside an alcove. (See also top left.)

decorative hardware

Faucets with cross handles and a gently arching spout look pretty in profile. (See also middle left.)

elegantly unfitted

Stone counters atop classically styled vanity cabinets reinforce the unfitted theme. (See also far left.)

handsome finish

The original wood floor was retained and refinished to match the room's furnishings. (See also left.)

design workbook
UNPRETENTIOUS AND APPEALING

simple good looks

Modern materials and finishes look fresh in this master bathroom. Light surfaces keep the space bright.

cast in concrete

Colored concrete was used for the tub deck and backsplash, left. The satin fittings, left, add a touch of glamour.

counter culture

Like the tub deck, the vanity countertop is concrete and has been sealed. (See also bottom far left.)

open storage

Open shelving underneath the vanity is an airy spot for extra towels and wash cloths. (See also middle left.)

matching metals

Chrome hardware in a satin finish was selected to match the bathroom faucets. (See also left.)

design workbook
ALONG MODERN LINES

not plain geometry

Cool and contemporary, the products and materials in this bath are sleek in form and texture. The repetition of lines plays up a modern sensibility.

function first

An adjustable showerhead that can also be hand held is a convenient feature for tall and not as tall members of the family. (See also far left.)

throw in a curve

Round wall-mounted lavs protrude past the face of the cabinetry and relieve the repetition of the many square shapes. (See also top left.)

pieces that gleam

Dazzling terrazzo tile, comprised of stone, glass, or other suitable chips that are embedded in cement, creates a multicolored floor pattern here. (See also left.)

design workbook

COOL IDEAS, WARM LOOK

less to stress about

Smooth surfaces, practical white fixtures, and sleek fittings make this room comfortable and easy to clean.

keep it simple

A no-frills concrete countertop has been installed over plain-panel cabinets. (See also top left.)

understated appeal

A modern high-arc faucet and a sprayer (mounted on the tub deck), middle left, are sleek and simple in design.

unobtrusive design

The one-piece low-profile toilet is compact and takes up little space in the corner. (See also bottom left.)

glass act

The glass doors of the large frameless medicine cabinet, far left, reflect additional light into the room.

7

style in your bath

Most homowners agree that a neutral scheme is the practical place to begin decorating a bathroom. But today's bathrooms have style and personality. Even if your starting point is with white or off-white fixtures and flooring, you can put a lot of pizzazz into the room with details that are easy and relatively inexpensive to modify as time goes by and fashions change. You can play it a little less safe in a small powder room because there's only a sink and toilet in terms of perma-nent fixtures. But whether your new bathroom comes together with the help of professionals or through your own efforts, it should express your style. Is your favorite color purple? Are you crazy for Art Deco? Are you a country lover, a city slicker, or a tradi-tionalist at heart? Approach this phase of the process with as much creative abandon as you can muster.

This comfortable, contempoary bathroom dis-plays a taste of yesteryear in the owners' choice of tub and fittings.

Favorite decorating themes or looks that you've incorporated into other rooms in the house can be carried over into the bath, if you like, using color, pattern, texture, and finishing materials that unify the overall decor. In this chapter you'll see a roundup of today's popular decorating styles, and you'll learn all you need to know to pull all of the elements together seamlessly into one coordinated scheme.

defining your style

Before locking yourself into one rigid style, remember the first rule of thumb about decorating: please yourself. While you may want to emulate a certain look, don't become a slave to it and squash your creative spirit along the way. The key is to build a room around a theme or a mood while carefully incorporating your personality into it. A favorite color is one good way to do this, or a repeated motif or pattern, which you can achieve with wallpaper or tile.

When considering style, most people need some inspiration. Think about rooms that you have admired and what attracted you. Was it a painted finish? A pretty fabric? Beautiful window treatments? Elegant cabinetry? Artful accessories? How did the room make you feel? Cheerful? Nostalgic? Restful? Energetic?

You can also take a clue from the rest of your home. Look at the architecture. Is it contemporary? Colonial or some other period style? Are there elaborate trimwork and ornamental details, or are the walls, doors, and windows streamlined and spare?

Even if the architecture is nondescript, you can introduce a period flavor with reproduction fixtures, window treatments, wallcoverings, and accessories. Is there a theme you have already established with the rest of your furnishings and decoration? Do you like antiques? Are you a collector, or someone who prefers a pared-down look? You can build on these features and preferences in the new bathroom or depart from them entirely if you wish. Find one transitional element, such as the floor treatment or the color scheme, to create a visual bridge so that the change from room to room isn't abrupt.

Whatever you do, your approach to decorating the new bath should be deliberate. Let it evolve over time. Don't rush your choices. Live with paint and wallpaper samples for a while, and make sure that you've sufficiently shopped around for good materials.

To help you discover what look is right for you, the following pages offer a brief description of popular decorating styles. Feel free to follow them or design a variation on one of these themes. Remember, colors, patterns, and other materials are suggestions. Use them as starting points, but let your own preferences guide you in the end.

LEFT
The Asian theme in this powder room is reinforced by the color selections, artwork, and choice of vanity and fixtures.

OPPOSITE
You can easily dress up and enliven a drab monochromatic bathroom through the use of fabric in rugs, shower curtains, and window treatments.

Traditional

Today's traditional style uses elements of English and American eighteenth- and early-nineteenth-century design. The look is rich and formal. Select wood cabinetry, finished in a mellow wood stain or painted white, with details like fluted panels, bullseye corner blocks, and dentil and crown molding. The cabinet's door style is usually a raised panel, sometimes slightly arched. Fabricate an elegant countertop with marble—or a plastic laminate that's a faux version. Hand-painted tiles work well, too. Hardware and fittings in polished brass will add a sophisticated Old World touch. Colors may include Wedgwood blue or deeply hued jewel tones. Patterns based on nature-inspired themes, such as flowers or birds, as well as formal stripes and tapestry or crewelwork look-alikes work well in traditional rooms. You might want to include an antique wardrobe in this bathroom for heirloom linens or nestle a Windsor chair next to the bath. Strictly speaking, success with traditional style lies in managing the details. Visit an architectural salvage shop to replace con-

temporary fixtures with gilded mirrors, wall sconces, and high-arched faucets, or shop for faithful reproductions. Install divided-light windows, and dress them with a formal window treatment, such as swags paired with drapery panels and sheers. For added privacy, use shutters or wood blinds along with your curtains.

ABOVE
The paneled tub platform, divided-light windows, chandelier, and detailed trimwork all spell an updated traditional style.

OPPOSITE
Another view of the bathroom above reinforces its traditional theme: raised-panel cabinetry and ornate detailing.

smart tip

TRADITIONAL STYLE

Retrofit an antique chest for bathroom storage, but make sure that you properly seal the wood against moisture. If you really want to be smart, buy a new cabinet that's made to look like an antique and won't fall prey to the assaults of humidity and water. Your old chest left open to display linens, soaps, and pretty bottled toiletries will create a focal point for the room.

Country

Call it pure Americana, English, Swedish, Italian, or French. The style is basic, casual, and warm—and every country has its own version. "Country" often implies a deeper connection with the outdoors and the simple life than other styles and uses an abundance of natural elements. Start with plain wood cabinetry stained a light maple, or add a distressed, crackled, or pickled finish. Door styles are usually framed, sometimes with a raised panel. Install a laminate countertop, and coordinate it with the tile you select for the room. Hand-painted tiles with a simple theme lend a custom touch.

For added country charm, stencil a wall border or select a wallpaper pattern with a folk-art motif or floral prints. Checks and ticking stripes are also popular in a country-style room—on the wall, as a tile pattern, or on the shower-curtain fabric. If you feel creative, apply a painted finish to the wall. Otherwise, check out the many wallpaper designs on the market that emulate the look of sponging, ragging, combing, and other special painted effects.

Install a double-hung window in the room. (Casement windows look too contemporary in this setting.) Some window treatment ideas include a balloon topper over mini blinds or shutters, for privacy, combined with a matching or contrasting lace café curtain. If you have a casement window in the bathroom that you do not want to change, install pop-in muntins to give the unit more of a traditional or old-fashioned look.

A skirted pedestal sink or pine chest-turned-vanity, along with reproduction faucets, will add a nostalgic charm to a country bathroom. Bring a playful note to this informal design with whimsical hardware fabricated in wrought iron, brushed pewter, or porcelain. Hardware and fittings that are polished look too refined for this style.

Popular country colors include red gingham and denim blue. Choose a checkerboard floor or a mosaic of broken tiles if hardwood is not available. Or consider laminate flooring that gives you the look of real wood without the maintenance. Some styles even come with a painted-floor design.

The country bath is the type of room that begs for baskets, old bottles, and ceramic vases filled with wildflowers. Accessorize with these items or a collection of favorite things, and you've created a very personal space.

LEFT
Somewhat short on square footage, this bathroom, with its French country blue vanity, displays the intimacy of country decor.

OPPOSITE
This vanity area is "a little bit country," with its white furnishings, simple lighting fixtures, and pale blue color scheme and flowers.

smart tip

COUNTRY STYLE
Collections are often part of a country decor, even in the bathroom. All you need is three or more of anything that have size, shape, or color in common. You can mass them on walls, on shelves, on the windowsills, or even along the edge of the tub.

Shaker

The basic tenants of the Shaker philosophy, which evolved out of a nineteenth-century religious movement, are built on a sense of humbleness. This is reflected in the way that Shakers designed their furniture and homes. They believed in using only the most essential elements, completely without ornamentation or frills. Their plain, practical, homespun designs featured dovetailed joints and hand-planed tops, plain panels on doors, and legs tapered almost to a pencil point. Finishes were always dyes or oils, never varnishes, to enhance the wood.

Contemporary cabinet manufacturers, responding to a renewed popularity of the Shaker look over the last decade, have used the Shakers' original designs to inspire similar updated versions of their own. When shopping for Shaker-style cabinetry for your new bath, look for the same plain paneled doors and wood finishes that are engineered to hold up against moisture. You can hang a matching medicine cabinet or install a mirror with a plain wood frame over the sink. A typical Shaker accessory is a slanted rack of shelves that can be freestanding or mounted to the wall. It works well in the room, acting as extra storage for towels and soaps. Place several round wooden Shaker stacking boxes on the shelves. You can find them unfinished in craft stores. Lightly sand them, and then apply paint in a color picked up from the woodwork.

Keeping simplicity in mind, paint the walls in your Shaker-inspired bath white or cream. Accent woodwork with a muted shade of slate blue, brick red, or harvest gold. Install plain fixtures in white or cream tones with unfussy fittings. Ceramic tile arranged in a quiltlike pattern can add more color accents and a reasonable amount of decoration.

A traditional double-hung window, with or without muntins, fits in fine with the Shaker theme. For privacy, hang plain wood shutters and panel-style curtains with tab tops that have been fabricated in simple cotton or muslin. A tin chandelier will pull the look together.

If there's room, place a Shaker-style ladder-back chair with a woven-tape seat in a corner of the room, and hang an old embroidered print on the wall.

smart tip

SHAKER STYLE

This warm, likable style fits in perfectly with a country home because of its old-fashioned values. But it blends in well with contemporary interiors, too, because of its clean lines and plain geometric shapes. In fact, adding a few Shaker elements can warm up the sometimes cold look of a thoroughly modern room.

OPPOSITE

Though not strictly Shaker by any means, this bathroom's inspiration is evident in the simple furniture design and lined basket.

BELOW

With its natural wood tones, rectilinear furniture, and woven seat, this lav/vanity area is closer to the Shaker aesthetic.

Contemporary

What we refer to as "contemporary style" evokes images of clean architectural lines, an absence of decoration and color, and materials like chrome, glass, and stone. Indeed, its roots are at the turn of the last century, when architects and designers flatly rejected the exaggerated artificial embellishments of the Victorians by turning to natural products and pared-down forms. Various modern movements, evolving over the course of the twentieth century, gradually incorporated new man-made materials into their streamlined forms. Hence the high-tech look popularized in the 1970s and 1980s.

Today, contemporary style is taking a softer turn, even in the bathroom, a place where hard edges, cool reflective surfaces, and cutting-edge technology abound. Bath designers are taking another look at time-honored forms and giving them a new spin. It's not unusual to see updated versions of traditional fixtures and fittings, for example, or new uses for natural materials in a contemporary bathroom. This is especially true as improved finishes have made these products more durable and easier to maintain. And although black and white are classic, the white palette identified with contemporary design over the last two decades has been replaced with earthy hues or warmer shades of white.

When selecting cabinets for your contemporary bath, pair a frameless door with a wood finish. Laminate cabinetry is still compatible with this style, but for an updated look, wood is it. For interest, don't be afraid to mix several materials and finishes on cabinets and other surfaces throughout the room. Combinations of wood and various metals, such as chrome, copper, brass, and pewter, make strong statements, as does the duo of stone and glass. Used on countertops or to fabricate the sink, shower, or tub surrounds, mixed materials keep the room from looking sterile. For more visual interest apply a glazed or textured finish to neutral-colored walls. And bring as much of the outdoors into this room as possible. Install casement-style windows and skylights or roof windows to blend with contemporary architecture. For privacy, use tailored Roman shades or vertical blinds on the windows.

ABOVE LEFT
This bathroom is unmistakably contemporary in its use of color, sleek fixtures and fittings, and abundant polished metal.

OPPOSITE
The use of marble, dark wood, and gold-plated lavatory and bath fixtures is emblematic of the extravagance of Neoclassicism.

Neoclassical

Neoclassical mimics the style of ancient Roman and Greek design. It developed in the late-eighteenth to mid-nineteenth century upon the excavation of the ruins of Pompeii and influenced furniture design of that era, including Federal and Empire styles. It is enjoying renewed popularity. Today's version incorporates classic architectural and design themes, including columns, pediments, ornate carvings and plasterwork, curvaceous shapes, and decorating motifs, such as urns, scrolls, and shield shapes. It is highly ornamental.

To achieve this opulent look, select formal-style wood cabinetry with heavy carving and ornate molding. Lavish the scheme with rich materials, such as a marble tub fabricated in one of a variety of white and pastel shades. Build the tub into a platform set off by columns. If solid marble or tiles are beyond your budget, opt for a look-alike in solid-surfacing material that can be used to form the tub, shower, sink, countertops, and even the bathroom floor.

Don't skimp on the details—this bath truly defines luxury. Go ahead and pamper yourself with gold-plated fittings and a chandelier. Install gilded sconces on either side of the vanity, and use accent lighting strips to draw attention to handsome details such as crown molding.

Colors that enhance the neoclassical look include white, off-white, black, gray, or gold, as well as earth tones such as sepia. Today, special painted effects and wallpaper that mimic stone (a throwback to those ancient stone villas) or soft, buttery leather pull everything together. Top it off with a wallpaper border or stencil that features an architectural motif or one that resembles swagged fabric.

An arched-top window suits a neoclassical bathroom perfectly. Dress it with a swag window treatment. For privacy, add either a Roman or pleated shade.

smart tip

NEOCLASSICAL STYLE

Instead of expensive hand-crafted plasterwork, look into the many prefabricated moldings, ceiling medallions, pillars, cornices, and the like that are made of lightweight molded plastic. They can be faux painted to resemble marble or stone and are fairly easy to install yourself.

Victorian

Anyone who likes nostalgia will appreciate this romantic, highly ornamented look. Think gingerbread; think lace. Use traditional-style, raised-panel doors painted white. Select cabinetry that features lots of decorative millwork, such as cutout panels. A graceful pedestal sink with a high-arc brass faucet or a lav with a pretty skirted bottom would be suitable in a Victorian setting. Choose antique fixtures and fittings in brass or a mixture of brass and porcelain, or shop for reproduction models. Well-known manufacturers offer a line of claw-footed tubs, pedestals, high-tank toilets, and the like to suit this decor. Some Victorian looks are very formal, with heavy patterns and lots of deep colors. Others are more casual and have a Victorian country-style appeal that combines light, airy colors with pretty, feminine curlicues, cutouts, and curves.

Black and white tiles set in a diamond pattern will fit right in here, as will wainscoting or molding painted a crisp white to match porcelain pieces. For lighting, include wall sconces and ceiling fixtures that mimic old gas lamps. A weathered wood floor will make this room cozy, too, especially topped with a charming hand-hooked rug.

On the wall, decorate with pretty wallpaper that features a floral motif or a complex paisley—two designs popular during the Victorian era. For an authentic look, mix more than one pattern. Don't be afraid of creating a mismatched mess. The trick to doing this successfully is sticking to the same colors—no matter how many different patterns you add to your decorating scheme.

For window treatments, select lace, such as a delicate Battenburg design. Carry this theme over to your shower curtain, too. For privacy, install a lace pleated shade or a ballon shade.

A small bamboo table or a white wicker piece always adds charm to rooms like this. If there's enough space, bring in a wicker vanity, shelves, or a small chair.

LEFT
You can almost smell the roses in this formal Victorian setting. The lace curtains, antique-look furniture-style vanity, heavily floral wallcovering, collectibles, and brass faucet and wall sconces all add to the atmosphere.

OPPOSITE
This modern throwback to pure Victoriana contains many of the most popular clues: claw-footed tub with brass feet, checkerboard tiles set on a diagonal, and heavily patterned wallcovering. The acrylic shower surround is a thoroughly modern touch.

smart tip

VICTORIAN STYLE
Victorian, today, is a very romantic look. To underscore this, add the scent of lavender or some other dried flower to the room or use potpourri, which you can keep in a bowl on the vanity. Hang a fragrant pomander on a hook; display lavender soaps on a wall shelf; or tuck sachets between towels on a shelf. For an authentic touch, display a Victorian favorite, the spider plant.

Arts and Crafts

The Arts and Crafts Movement, with roots at the turn of the twentieth century, was a reaction to the ornamentation of Victorian design and the growing use of machines to produce cheap goods. It also professed a philosophy that beautiful, simple, organic objects arranged harmoniously in a house will contribute to one's well-being. The movement's aesthetic is enjoying a resurgence today. Styles that are related to or part of the Arts and Crafts Movement include Mission, Craftsman, and Prairie (Frank Lloyd Wright's signature style).

Start with plain oak cabinets with a hand-crafted appearance. As with Shaker style, manufacturers are responding to the public interest in Arts and Crafts style today, and some offer a line of authentically inspired cabinets. Accessorize with hand-hammered copper hardware. If you can't find genuine examples, shop for reproductions.

smart tip

ARTS AND CRAFTS STYLE

The heart of this style rests in its earthy connection. The more you can bring nature into it, the more authentic it will be. An easy way to do this is with plants. A bonus is that plants naturally thrive in the bathroom where they enjoy the humid environment.

The more wood, the better in an Arts and Crafts-style room. Oil the wood well to bring out the grain, and properly seal it against water damage.

For the walls, combine an tall oak wainscot with a stylized wallpaper—one that combines floral motifs within a geometric pattern. There are wallpaper manufacturers who specialize in this style. Select colors that reflect the hues of nature, such as brown, green, blue, and orange. Accessorize with organically shaped pottery in these colors. Pull it together by incorporating native American textiles into this motif, too.

For tile, select natural colors and textures or ones with matte or "art pottery" glazes, such as crystalline. Lighting fixtures can include a combination of unobtrusive recessed canisters and wall fixtures with Tiffany-style glass covers or mica shades. You may want to include a Mission-style chair or small table in the room. If so, make sure that the wood isn't exposed to moisture.

Plain windows should be curtained very simply in an Arts and Crafts-style room, using natural fabrics, such as linen or muslin, with an embroidered border. Typical motifs include gingko leaves and poppy seeds. Preferably, instead of traditional treatments, use stained-glass or art-glass windows, which will provide both privacy and a dramatic play of light. There are several manufacturers today that produce an Arts and Crafts line of stained-glass windows.

LEFT
The subtle decorating choices made in this bathroom point to Arts and Crafts: high wainscot, earthy color scheme, wood appointments, and etched shower door in the Prairie style.

OPPOSITE
Typical of the Art and Crafts style, the abundance of warm wood and tilework in this bathroom creates a space with a serene, relaxing atmosphere.

Art Deco

Dramatic and a bit exotic, Art Deco is the forerunner of modern design. It evolved during the first two decades of the twentieth century. Hallmarks include a flamboyant use of geometric shapes, pastel colors, and lots of chrome.

In today's Art Deco-influenced bathroom, start with contemporary cabinetry. A vanity with a rounded or tubular-shape front and frameless doors is perfect. For countertop material, check out stainless steel, chrome, or glass, or install a solid-surfacing material with a bullnose edge. Hang a round frameless mirror above the sink. Streamlined fixtures and reproduction chrome faucets from the 1920s and 1930s will look great in an Art Deco-style bath. Accent with color, especially in tiles designed in a geometric pattern, such as a zigzag or a sunburst. Black and

white are the basic tones to begin with; then add blasts of bright pastels, such as pinks, corals, and turquoise.

This is a look that can be serious or playful. For inspiration, look at pictures of early twentieth-century Miami architecture, much of which still exists, or the great ocean liners of pre World War II.

the decorating phase

Once you've determined the style that suits your personality, you can begin to take the steps that will pull together the entire project. Remember, using a particular style as a guide is helpful, but listen to your own instincts when decorating. Begin the decorating phase of your bath project by following these simple steps:

smart tip

ART DECO STYLE

One thing you don't want in an Art Deco room is ornament. You can mix elements of contemporary style with this look, however. To give this room interest, rely on lots of sleek shiny surfaces. Apply a lacquered finish to cabinetry. Display prints in glossy lacquered frames painted in bright pastel colors. Use chrome accessories, such as soap dishes, vases, and towel bars.

smart steps
stylish decorating

Step 1 CREATE A SAMPLE BOARD
Don't make your bathroom decorating all trial and error. Try out your ideas on a sample board first. To make one, use a piece of $\frac{1}{2}$-inch plywood, which is heavy enough to hold your samples but light enough for you to handle. Mount your samples—paint chips, fabric swatches, flooring and tile samples, countertop chips, and any other material you plan to bring into the room—on the board to see how each one works as part of an overall scheme. The larger the sample, the better. If a wallpaper pattern clashes with the color or pattern of the tile, change one or both until you find a match. The board lets you test ideas before

you start buying materials and make costly mistakes.

Try different combinations of colors and patterns. Look at them under all types of light, night and day. Add photographs of fixtures or materials you may want to include in the room but don't have samples of to put on the board.

Create a cheat sheet, based on your sample boards, to take with you when shopping. Your sample board is a wonderful resource for building a room that works together in harmony. (Note: Remembering color shade accurately is nearly impossible. Working without a

guide is a sure way to end up with something that doesn't match.)

When creating your sample board, include your sources. Note store names for every item, as well as manufacturers. If there are model numbers and color names, write them down, too. This will be invaluable if you ever have to do a touchup or replace an item in the room later. Your sample board also may come in handy if you decide to redecorate adjoining rooms. With all your samples, it won't be so difficult to achieve a cohesive or compatible style.

Step 2 NOTE THE SIGHT LINES

A sight line is the visual path the eye follows from a given point within a room or from an entrance. A room's primary sight line is at the entry. It is the most important one because it draws your attention into the room. Your eye immediately moves in one direction toward whatever is directly opposite the doorway. Very often in a bathroom that focus will be the tub, but it could be the toilet. Hopefully, it's not. The time for relocating fixtures is not at the decorating stage. However, if you're still in the planning process and reading this chapter for ideas, you should review the fixture placements in your base map and look over Chapter Two, "Designing a Smart Layout."

Once you're inside a room, there are other sight lines to consider. In today's spalike bathing environments, they have become more significant because people spend more time in the bathroom, whether to read, relax, exercise, or even socialize. Begin noting sight lines at the tub area. What will you face when you're sitting in it? Who wouldn't enjoy a bubble bath next to a pretty view to the outdoors? If that's not a possibility, looking at attractive wall art is better than staring at the toilet.

Move to other places in the bathroom where you are apt to linger. Examine all of the sight lines reflected in any mirrors, not just the one over the vanity. Contemporary bathrooms, particularly spacious master baths, can contain a lot of mirrored and glass surfaces that draw attention to things that might otherwise go unnoticed, such as piping under a pedestal sink, the toilet area, or dead corners. Think about how you want to move your eye around the room, too. Sight lines should be fluid. You don't want your eye to jump from one element to the next. You want it to move from the curve of the sink up to the roundness of the mirror, for example. Use repeated color and pattern to create a rhythm that will carry your vision from one place to the next. If there are a lot of boxy corners that stop the flow, introduce a few curved or rounded shapes around the room. When you want to draw attention to something, highlight it with a color that contrasts with the rest of the room or accent it with light. On the other hand, you can play down an unattractive feature or sight line using the same devices for diverting the eye elsewhere.

Sight lines in the home are the same as lines in a painting or in a graphic design. What pulls the eye should be continuous. Find balance and symmetry in your sight lines. Don't place all of the most powerful visual elements on one side of the room. Plan some way to attract attention to the farthest corners and the most uninspired sections of the room. It could be the addition of a single accessory that does the trick. Fill a basket with colorful towels or soaps, or artfully arrange a collection of anything on a wall.

OPPOSITE
The dramatic tub and window draw the eye first, but the double vanity picks up quickly.

ABOVE
The placement of the mirror, vanity, and chair creates a pleasing symmetry that draws you in.

Step 3 ADD DETAILS

More than anything else, it is the details in a room that people react to and remember—the Shaker pegged towel rack or the curlicued wicker chair. Details have a powerful effect on the feeling or mood of the room, too. They usually make the difference between a room that looks professionally designed and one that lacks polish. With details, you are bringing personality and something of yourself into the space.

Some of the best details you can include are the smallest—drawer pulls you picked up at an antique store, an old mantle you found at an architectural salvage yard that makes the perfect shelf above the toilet in the powder room, pretty shells in a glass jar or just left on the countertop.

No matter how big or small the room, details will pull the style together. Add period flavor with crown molding. Dress up contemporary fixtures with polished stone fittings. Display items you like in artful ways on the walls, shelves, or countertop. Don't worry if it's a collection of disparate objects, sizes, and shapes. Anything connected by a theme will work. Different prints in the same frame or with the same matting will do. Mix photographs with paintings or other odd objects. Group things for impact, such as a collection of candles near the tub for a candlelit soak. Display your favorite holiday momentos, kids art, or odd pieces of old china in the room.

When arranging, keep scale and proportion in mind. A large object on a small surface looks awkward; a small object on large surface looks odd, too. When grouping things, balance one large object with several small ones. Practice your arrangements on the floor before hanging them, or sketch them to scale on paper first.

OPPOSITE LEFT AND RIGHT
The detail's in the tile. Here, colorful tile accents (left) and an unusual border in the mosaic floor tiles (right) give the rooms the extra spark that says, "Look at me." The "sea" theme in the rooms is reinforced by collected artifacts.

BELOW LEFT AND RIGHT
Strong geometrical shapes in browns and whites are juxtaposed with the translucent, jewel-like violet vessel sink (left). The unusual mirror and collectible glass pieces on the counter in this pleasant bathroom (right) signal a playful personality behind its decor.

Step 4 USE COLOR

Color is probably your greatest decorating tool. Don't be afraid of it—it also happens to be one of the easiest things to change. So why do people typically stick with a neutral palette in the bathroom? A dated color on a permanent fixture can be expensive to replace if you're replacing the entire fixture. However, new paints make it possible to refurbish ceramic and porcelain with a new color for a fraction of the cost of replacement.

If you still want to stick with white or beige for the tub, sink, and toilet, introduce color to the walls or with accessories. Just pick up a can of paint and see how color can transform the space in no time at all. If you don't like what you've done, just grab another can of paint and start again. It's inexpensive and easy to apply.

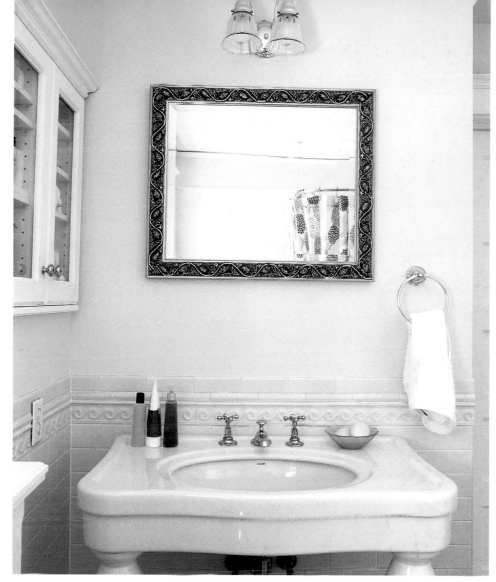

One of the simplest things that you can do to test out a color is to apply it to a sheet of white poster board, hang it on the wall, and live with it a few days. Look at it during the day; then wait for evening and look at it again under varying levels of artificial light. Is the color still appealing to you? What effect does it have on the space at different times of the day? Even if you're thinking about tiling a wall or installing wallpaper, pick out the dominant color, find a matching paint, and apply this simple test.

Color has amazing properties. It can evoke memories, create a mood, or even change your perception of space. Light colors expand a room, darker colors draw the walls inward. This is also true of ceilings. If you have a high ceiling that seems out of proportion to the small measurements of the room, you may want to paint it a dark color for contrast and to force the perspective in the room. What you are doing is creating an optical illusion.

As a rule of thumb, use no more than three colors in one room. There really can be too much of a good thing. Use the colors in unique amounts and, perhaps, in different shades and tints. A monochromatic (one color) scheme will produce a calming effect. Unfortunately, it can also appear dull and uninspired. You can counteract the monotony of one color by using it in various shades, textures, and patterns. One easy way to accomplish this is with a painted finish like ragging, sponging, or glazing.

OPPOSITE
Introduce strong color choices in accessories such as towels and shower curtains. Using white or neutral in fixtures and permanent wall treatments like tiles ensures longevity through periodic changes in color taste and sensibility.

ABOVE RIGHT
Pleasing, warm sunshine yellow stands out against the white lavatory and wall tile and makes a bright impression.

The stronger a color, the less of it is used. That's another general rule, which can be broken by your personal preference, of course. A dollop of saturated red equals an entire wall of pale pink in visual weight.

When you use two or three colors, combine unequal amounts and different shades of each one along with a dash of black, white, or another neutral. If you don't, your eyes won't know where to focus. Let one color dominate.

Anchor your accent colors in opposite parts of the room. For example, you can pick up a color from the wallpaper in the towels hanging by the tub, and then use the same color in a vase on the vanity countertop.

Where do you get your color inspiration? Forget about color fads. Look at the world around you. For an explosion of color, visit the produce aisle of the grocery store. Comb through fashion magazines and art books.

Look at your own closet! Tear out pictures of anything with color that attracts and pleases you. Keep a record in your design notebook. After you've got a stack of these tear sheets, divide them up by color. Whatever color dominates that collection is a good indicator of what pleases you most of the time.

BELOW
The use of one strong color in an otherwise monochromatic bathroom makes a bold statement.

OPPOSITE
Rules are made to be broken. This bathroom's walls are painted an intense red hue, which is usually reserved as an accent color.

wallpaper, paint, and fabric

OPPOSITE
The understated pattern in the muted wallcovering plays ever so subtly off the strong color of the vanity cabinetry, mirror, and window casing and shutters.

ABOVE
The rustic brick wall complements the fish-themed wallcovering and picture to create a decidedly masculine environment in this large, airy bathroom.

While you're thinking about color for the new bathroom, consider the type of paint, wallpaper, and fabric to use. Remember, bathrooms have lots of glossy surfaces, which reflect light. Unless you want an intense effect, opt for low-luster paints and matte finishes. If you are concerned about moisture, especially in a room without a duct vent, shop for products that have been treated with mildewcide in the manufacturing process. Moist areas are perfect breeding grounds for mold. When moisture seeps behind wallpaper, it creates a moldy, peeling mess. Luckily, this is a problem that can be avoided because you'll find that there is a widely available selection of products and glues that are designed specifically for bathroom applications.

After you've settled on a color scheme, you can look for wallpaper and fabrics to carry your theme through. Use them, later, to pick up a solid color for accents or trim. Two major factors in deciding the patterns to choose are the location and size of the room. Review the sight lines from outside of the bathroom. Look at the adjoining areas, especially the ones that you must pass through to get to the bathroom. Think of them sequentially. Ideally, you should create an interrelationship between all the patterns and colors that run from room to room. If you want stripes in the bath but the adjoining hallway has a floral wallpaper, match the colors. In a small bathroom, as a rule, a bold print may be too busy. On the other hand, it may be just what is needed to make a large space feel cozier. Vertical designs will add height to a room. Conversely, horizontal motifs will draw the eye around it. In general, patterned wallpaper looks best in a traditional-style room. In a contemporary setting, subtle patterns that don't detract from the architecture and the materials are best. And always avoid trendy looks, unless you want to make changes every couple of years.

Lastly, texture is a way to bring visual interest to the bathroom. Some paints and papers come with a textured finish, or you can create your own illusion of one with special techniques, such as sponging, ragging, graining, and combing. Simple do-it-yourself kits are inexpensive and available at home centers, hardware stores, and craft shops. If you're not in the painting mood, there are wallpaper patterns that are printed to look like these effects.

design workbook
BEAUTY IS IN THE DETAILS

tile art

Custom tile treatments like this "work of art," which is created in mosaic tile with gold accents and is located in the shower, are decorative details that also provide interest in the bathroom design. (See also top left.)

collections

Strategically placed collections of decorative soaps, sponges, candles, lotions, and the like add personality and a touch of whimsy to bathroom decor. (See also left.)

subtle details

Using small accents like these in the floor tile treatment provides your bathroom with a level of detail that makes it special.

design workbook
CONTEMPORARY ECLECTICISM

modern brightwork

Gleaming fittings and exposed pipework are emblematic of a contemporary decorating treatment. (See also top left and bottom left and right.)

eye relief

Works of art, groupings of collectibles, and flowers provide points of interest and relief from the starkness of a contemporary decor.

focal points

When you first enter this monochromatic bath, the furniture is the first thing to catch your eye. A large bathroom allows you to use objects you might not otherwise include.

monochromatic color

You can get a monochromatic look, at home in contemporary decor, by using the same color but different textures on the floor and walls.

design workbook
VICTORIAN POWDER ROOM

ornament

Highly decorative accessories, such as these crystal-draped sconces and highly orna-mented bird-motif mirror, are hallmarks of a Victorian decorat-ing style. (See also top left.)

collectibles

Display collected items in small groupings to give a sense of per-sonality to your bathroom. The collections add a point of interest to the room, giv-ing it that extra level of detail that can make all the difference.

period furniture

Unmistakably Victorian, with its detailed relief patterns and elaborate, deli-cately curving brasswork legs, the vanity and carved-stone ves-sel lavatory look as if they would be right at home in the boudoir of a woman from the period. (See also left.)

design workbook
ARTS AND CRAFTS AESTHETIC

compartmentalization

Dividing the bathroom floor space according to task makes sense, especially in a shared space. Here the vanity area is separated from the bathing and toilet area to make the daily routine run more smoothly.

colorful touch

Bright flowers, fresh or faux, add a touch of color to brighten the morning routine in a bathroom with an otherwise muted color pallette.

woven arts

Wood floors are right at home in an Arts and Crafts environment, but even more so hand-woven rugs that exhibit the aesthetic of North American artwork. (See also top left and left.)

design workbook
RUSTIC SHAKER-STYLE AUSTERITY

simple adornments

The Shaker aesthetic of simple living is evident in this bathroom, which almost looks as if it came right out of a nineteenth-century cabin. Wrought-iron accessories like sconces are at home here. (See also top left.)

portable practicality

Baskets are big in Shaker living. They are wonderful for organizing; they can be easily cleaned out; and they are portable, so you can put them where you need them. This basket and the stool act as "linen closets."

re-creations

Take away the faucet, and the rustic vanity and white vessel sink look authentically nineteenth century. (See also left.) The simple table and spartan window treatments are typical of Shaker-style design.

design workbook
MODERN TRADITION

touch of class

The gilded mirror is an elegant focal point. Note how the "back-splash" follows its contour.

coordinating colors

When using a wallcovering, coordinate the colors and pattern with the color scheme in the rest of the room. (See also bottom left.)

durable surfaces

Marble and acrylic marble are traditional countertop surfaces for bathroom vanities.

painted wood

When using wood in the bathroom, be sure it is painted or sealed well against moisture.

accent pieces

Small pieces of furniture, top left and far left, are perfect as accents in a bathroom.

design workbook
EXOTIC CONTEMPORARY

dramatic lighting

The use of down-lighting for general illumination in this bath produces a dramatic effect by emphasizing the texture of the walls. (See also top left.)

textured walls

The walls are made from smooth river rock that is adhered to mesh backing to form sheets, similar to mosaic tile. (See also bottom far left.)

signature sink

The painted earthenware vessel sink makes a dramatic statement, looking like an antique wash basin in a thoroughly modern setting. (See also left.)

custom countertop

The "vanity" and extended ledge are custom-made from thick blocks of solid clear acrylic for a unique contemporary look. (See also left.)

design workbook
GOING TO GREAT HEIGHTS

vaulted ceilings

Today's luxury bathrooms are larger than ever before, and with the extra square footage often comes extra height: ceilings tend to be taller than ever, too. Homeowners and designers look to these higher ceilings for extra visual impact, so they try different shapes, like the barrel-vaulted ceiling in this-bathroom, which is a modern take on traditional style. The ceiling is covered by decorative tile arranged in geometric shapes for added impact. (See also top left.) Other dramatic ceiling treatments include tray ceilings and stepped ceilings. (See left and far left, respectively.)

8

project timeline

As you consider your bathroom remodeling project, remember that every contractor works differently, and each job is unique. However, there are common steps that divide up the process into logical sequences that eventually result in a finished bathroom.

Here's a timeline of events that will help you to gauge—in a sequential fashion—the work that is involved. The estimated time lengths indicated here for the various stages are for an average-sized bathroom using standard products and materials. Keep in mind that the times shown are approximate, and depending on the scope of your project, they may actually be shorter or longer. Plus, you should be aware that things often happen on the jobsite that stall the work unexpectedly. In general, however, you can expect your new bathroom within a couple of months.

The more elaborate a job, the longer it will take. Plan carefully, especially when ordering custom-made materials.

smart steps
project scheduling

■ **Step 1** PREPLANNING
- ■ Make the decision to remodel.
- ■ Assess the problems and goals involved.
- ■ Gather ideas, and review trends.
- ■ Develop a budget, and obtain financing.
- ■ Collect information about contractors.
- ■ Arrange interviews with contractors.
- ■ Select a contractor.

■ **Step 3** DESIGN AND AGREEMENT
- ■ Meet with the designer for presentation of preliminary drawings and project specifications.
- ■ Review and discuss options.
- ■ Sign a design agreement.

4 WEEKS	1 WEEK	2–3 WEEKS	2–4 WEEKS

■ **Step 2** INITIAL MEETINGS
- ■ Walk through the existing space.
- ■ Brainstorm with the contractor.
- ■ Decide whether the project is feasible within the budget.
- ■ Sign a letter of intent if you're purchasing design services, or skip to step 4.

■ **Step 4** DESIGN DEVELOPMENT
- ■ Review completed drawings and project notes.
- ■ Clarify any misunderstandings about the scope and intent of the project.
- ■ Select products.
- ■ Sign the construction contract.
- ■ Make the first down payment.
- ■ Wait three days for the Right of Recision period to pass, if applicable.
- ■ Obtain permits.
- ■ Meet with the construction team, and sign a preconstruction agreement.

Step 5 AFTER PERMITS ARE ISSUED
- Order products.
- Finalize the project schedule, and distribute it.
- Discuss the impact of the project on home life with the family, including safety issues and keeping pets out of the workplace.
- Remove personal items and breakables from the construction area.

Step 7 FINAL STAGES
- Inspect the job, and establish a list of final details to make sure everything is completed to your satisfaction.
- Obtain the final inspection and certificate of occupancy or habitability.
- Make a substantial completion payment.

| 1 WEEK | 4–8 WEEKS | 1 WEEK | 1 WEEK |

Step 6 THE WORK
- Complete the demolition.
- Complete the framing.
- Rough-in mechanical systems.
- Install the drywall.
- Install the flooring.
- Install the cabinetry.
- Install fixtures.
- Do the finishing work (painting and wallpapering).

Step 8 THE CONCLUSION
- Give the final approval.
- Make the final payment.

appendix BATH TEMPLATES

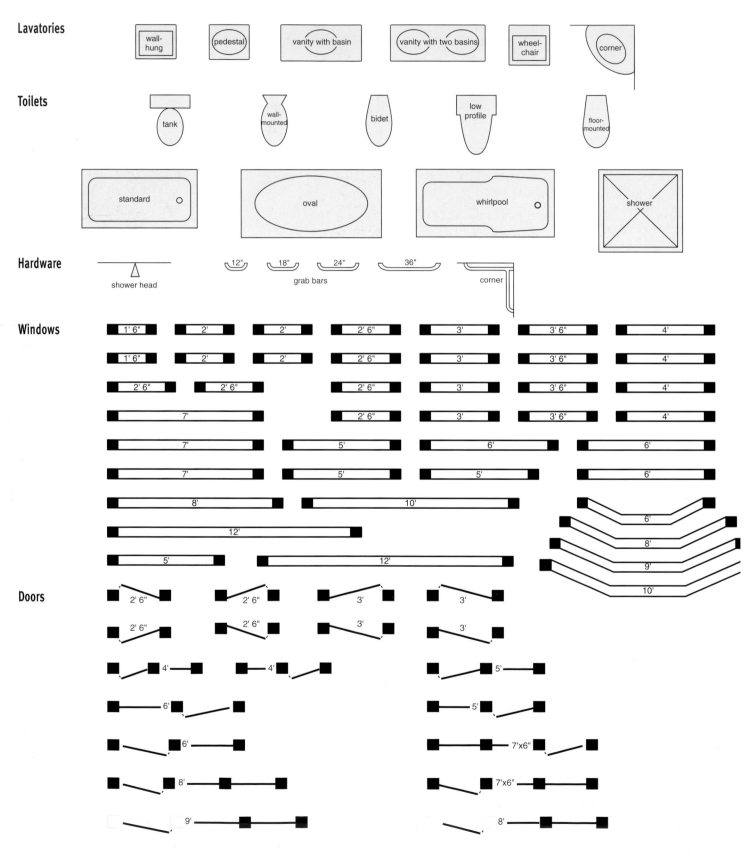

Lavatories

Toilets

Hardware

Windows

Doors

Scale: 1 square=1 foot

basic bathroom PLANNING GUIDELINES

According to the National Kitchen & Bath Association (NKBA), there are over 40 million pre-existing houses in the United States. Very often, these homes contain a typical-sized 5- x 7-foot bathroom. That doesn't leave much space for more than a standard tub, toilet, and lavatory, so professional designers encourage remodelers to expand these small baths to accommodate more amenities and to provide greater space for maneuvering safely and comfortably. The NKBA has developed a comprehensive list of bathroom planning guidelines that help both bath design professionals and homeowners who are designing a bath remodel on their own—whether or not expansion is an option. These guidelines appear here with the expressed permission of the NKBA.

1a. Doorways at least 32 inches wide and not more than 24 inches deep in the direction of travel.

1b. The clear space at a doorway must be measured at the narrowest point.

1c. Walkways should be a minimum of 36 inches wide.

2. Clear floor space at least the width of the door on the push side and a larger clear floor space on the pull side for maneuvering to open, close, and pass through the doorway.

3. A minimum clear floor space of 30 x 48 inches either parallel or perpendicular should be provided at the lavatory.

4a. A minimum clear floor space of 48 x 48 inches provided in front of the toilet with 16 inches of that clear floor space extending to each side of the fixture's centerline.

4b. Up to 12 inches of the 48 x 48 inches of clear floor space can extend under the lavatory when total access to a knee space is provided.

5. A minimum clear floor space of 48 x 48 inches from the front of the bidet should be provided.

6a. A minimum clear floor space of 60 x 30 inches at the bathtub for a parallel approach.

6b. A minimum clear floor space of 60 x 48 inches at the bathtub for a perpendicular approach.

7. A minimum clear floor space at a shower less than 60 inches wide should be 36 inches deep x shower width + 12 inches. A shower 60 inches wide or greater requires a space of 36 inches deep x shower width.

8. The clear floor spaces required at each fixture may overlap.

9. Turning space of 180 degrees planned for in the bathroom. Minimum diameter of 60 inches for 360-degree turns and/or T-turn with a space of 36 x 36 x 60 inches.

10. A minimum clear floor space of 30 x 48 inches is required beyond the door swing in the bathroom.

11. For more than one vanity, one may be 30–34 inches and another 34–42 inches high.

12. Kneespace provided at the lavatory, 27 inches above the floor at the front edge and 30 inches wide.

13. The bottom edge of the mirror over the lavatory should be a maximum of 40 inches above the floor or a maximum of 48 inches above the floor if it is tilted.

14. The minimum clear floor space from the centerline of the lavatory to any side wall is 15 inches.

15. The minimum clearance between two bowls in the lavatory center is 30 inches, centerline to centerline.

16. In an enclosed shower, the minimum usable interior dimensions are 34 x 34 inches measured wall to wall.

17. Showers should include a bench or seat that is 17–19 inches above the floor and a minimum of 15 inches deep.

18. A 60-inch shower requires a 32-inch entrance. If the shower is 42 inches deep, 36 inches is required.

19. Shower doors must open into the bathroom.

20. No steps at the tub or shower area. Safety rails should be installed to facilitate transfer.

21. All showerheads equipped with a pressure-balance/temperance regulator or temperature-limiting device.

22a. Shower controls accessible from inside and outside the fixture and located between 38–48 inches above the floor and offset toward the room.

22b. Tub controls accessible from inside and outside the fixture and located between the tub rim and 33 inches above the floor, below the grab bar and offset toward room.

23a. A minimum 16-inch clearance from the centerline of the toilet or bidet to any obstruction on either side.

23b. For adjacent toilet and bidet installation, the 16-inch minimum clearance to all obstructions should be maintained.

24. The toilet-paper holder installed within reach of person seated on the toilet, slightly in front of the edge of the toilet and centered 26 inches above the floor.

25. Compartmentalized toilet areas should be a minimum of 36 x 66 inches with a swing-out door or pocket door.

26. Walls reinforced to receive grab bars in the tub, shower, and toilet areas.

27. Storage for toiletries, linens, grooming, and general bathroom supplies provided 15–48 inches above the floor.

28. Storage for soap, towels, and personal hygiene items should be installed within reach of person seated on bidet or toilet or within 15–48 inches above the floor and do not interfere with use of fixture.

29. In the tub/shower area, storage for soap and personal hygiene items provided with 15–48 inches above the floor.

30. All flooring should be slip-resistant.

31. Exposed pipes and mechanicals covered by protective panel or shroud.

32. Controls, dispensers, outlets, and operating mechanisms 15–48 inches above the floor and operable with a closed fist.

33. Access panel to all mechanical, electrical, and plumbing systems.

34. Mechanical ventilation systems included to vent entire room. Calculation for minimum size of system: Cubic space (L x W x H) x 8 (changes per hour) = minimum cubic feet per minute (CFM) 60 minutes

35. Ground fault circuit interrupters specified on all receptacles, lights, and switches. All light fixtures above the tub/shower must be moisture-proof, special-purpose fixtures.

36. Auxiliary heating may be planned in addition to the primary heat source.

37. Every function should be well illuminated with task lighting, night lights, and/or general lighting. No lighting fixtures should be within reach of person seated or standing in tub or shower.

38. Bathroom lighting should include a window/skylight area equal to a minimum of 10 percent of bathroom's square footage.

39. Controls, handles, and door/drawer pulls should be operable with one hand, require minimal strength, and do not require tight grasp, pinching, or twisting of wrist.

40. Use clipped or radius corners for open countertops and eased to eliminate sharp edges.

41. Any glass in a tub/shower partition or other glass application within 18 inches of the floor should be laminated glass with a plastic interlayer, tempered glass, or approved plastic.

resource guide

The following list of manufacturers and associations is meant to be a general guide to additional industry and product-related sources. It is not intended as a listing of products and manufacturers represented by the photographs in this book.

Accessible Environments, Inc.
6893 Bellroi Rd.
Gloucester, VA 23061
Phone: 800-643-5906
www.acessinc.com
Sells handicap-accessible products

American Standard
P.O. Box 6820
1 Centennial Plaza
Piscataway, NJ 08855-6820
www.americanstandard-us.com
Manufactures plumbing and tile products

Ann Sacks Tile & Stone, a division of Kohler
8120 NE 33rd Dr.
Portland, OR 97211
Phone: 800-278-8453
www.annsacks.com
Manufactures ceramic, glass, and stone tile

Armstrong World Industries
2500 Columbia Ave.
P.O. Box 3001
Lancaster, PA 17604
Phone: 800-233-3823
www.armstrong.com
Manufactures floors, cabinets, and ceilings

Artistic Tile
79 5th Ave.
New York, NY 10003
Phone: 800-260-8646
www.artistictile.com
Offers diffferent types of tile, including those made of stone, ceramic, glass, metal, cement, and cork

BainUltra (also known as Ultra Bath)
956 Chemin Olivier
Saint-Nicolas, QC
Canada G7A 2N1
Phone: 800-463-2187
www.ultrabath.com
Manufactures a luxury line of bathtubs that offer a hydro-therapeutic massage

Benjamin Moore
51 Chestnut Ridge Rd.
Montvale, NJ 07645
Phone: 800-344-0400
www.benjaminmoore.com
Manufactures paint

Cooper Lighting
1121 Hwy. 74 S.
Peachtree City, GA 30269
Phone: 708-956-8400
www.cooperlighting.com
Manufactures lighting products

Corian, a division of DuPont
Chestnut Run Plaza
721 Maple Run
P.O. Box 80721
Wilmington, DE 19880
Phone: 800-426-7426
www.corian.com
Manufactures solid-surfacing material for home and commercial baths and kitchens

Dal-Tile
7834 C. F. Hawn Fwy.
Dallas, TX 75217

Phone: 888-933-8453
www.daltile.com
Manufactures ceramic and stone tile

Dex Studios
Phone: 404-753-0600
www.dexstudios.com
Creates custom concrete sinks, tubs, and countertops

Eisenhart Wallcoverings
400 Pine St.
Hanover, PA 17331
Phone: 800-555-2554
www.eisenhartwallcoverings.com
Manufactures wallpaper and borders for the home

Formica Coporation
225 E. 5th St.
Suite 200
Cincinatti, OH 45202
Phone: 800-367-6422
www.formica.com
Manufactures plastic laminate and solid-surfacing material

HEWI
3901 Cheyenne Dr.
P.O. Box 4000
Archdale, NC 27263-4000
Phone: 800-423-3531
www.hewi.com
Manufactures bathroom hardware and accessories

Grohe
14801 Quorum Dr., Ste. 550
Dallas, TX 75254
Phone: 800-444-7643
www.grohe.com
Manufactures bathroom and kitchen faucets and shower systems

Jacuzzi Whirlpool Bath
2121 N. California Blvd.
Walnut Creek, CA 94596
Phone: 800-288-4002
www.jacuzzi.com
Manufactures luxury tubs and showers for the home

Kohler
444 Highland Dr.
Kohler, WI 53044
Phone: 800-456-4537
www.kohlerco.com
Manufactures sinks, lavs, faucets, tubs, and accessories

KraftMaid Cabinetry
P.O. Box 1055
Middlefield, OH 44062
Phone: 888-562-7744
www.kraftmaid.com
Manufactures stock and built-to-order cabinetry

Lasco
8101 E. Kaiser Blvd.
Anaheim, CA 92808
Phone: 800-945-2726
www.lascobathware.com
Offers products including barrier-free showers

Lightolier
631 Airport Rd.
Fall River, MA 02720
Phone: 800-215-1068
www.lightolier.com
Manufactures lighting fixtures

Majestic Shower Company
1795 Yosemite Ave.
San Francisco, CA 94124
Phone: 800-675-6225
www.majesticshower.com
Manufactures showers and glass-door enclosures

Mannington, Inc.
75 Mannington Mills Rd.
Salem, NJ 08079
Phone: 800-482-9527
www.mannington.com
Manufactures residential and commercial flooring products

Mansfield Plumbing Products
150 1st St.
Perrysville, OH 44864
Phone: 877-850-3060
www.mansfieldplumbing.com
Manufactures toilets, lavs, bathtubs, and whirlpools

Merillat Industries
5353 West U.S. 223
P.O. Box 1946
Adrian, MI 49221
Phone: 800-575-8763
www.merillat.com
Manufactures bath and kitchen cabinetry

National Association of the Remodeling Industry (NARI)
780 Lee St., Ste. 200
Des Plaines, IL 60016
Phone: 800-611-6274
www.nari.org
A trade association for remodeling professionals; provides educational programs as well as online information for both professionals and consumers

National Kitchen and Bath Association (NKBA)
687 Willow Grove St.
Hackettstown, NJ 07840
Phone: 800-843-6522
www.nkba.org
A trade organization for kitchen and bath specialists; provides remodeling information, programs, and business tools to professionals and homeowners

Moen
25300 Al Moen Dr.
North Olmstead, OH 44070
Phone: 800-289-6636
www.moen.com
Manufactures faucets, sinks, and accessories for the bath and kitchen

NuTone
4820 Red Bank Rd.
Cincinatti, OH 45227
Phone: 888-336 3948
www.nutone.com
Manufactures exhaust fans, ceiling fans, heaters, and indoor-air quality products

Motif Designs
20 Jones St.
New Rochelle, NY 10802
Phone: 800-431-2424
www.motif-designs.com
Manufactures furniture, fabrics, and wallcoverings

Ondine, a part of Interbath, Inc.
665 N. Baldwin Park Blvd.
City of Industry, CA 91746
Phone: 800-423-9485
www.interbath.com/ondine
Manufactures luxury shower systems

Mr. Sauna, Inc., and **Mr. Steam, Inc.,** part of the Sussman
Lifestyle Group
43–20 34th St.
Long Island City, NY 11101
Phone: 800-767-8326
www.mrsauna.com, www.mrsteam.com
Manufacture sauna heaters; pre-cut, pre-built, and custom saunas; steam and aroma steam generators; and acrylic and fiberglass enclosures

Price Pfister, Inc.
19701 Da Vinci
Foothill Ranch, CA 92610
Phone: 800-732-8238
www.pricepfister.com
Manufactures faucets

Phone: 800-336-1110
www.sherwinwilliams.com
Manufactures paint and other coatings

Sonoma Cast Stone
P.O. Box 1721
Sonoma, CA 95476
Phone: 888-807-4234
www.sonomastone.com
Designs and builds concrete sinks and countertops

Sterling Plumbing
2900 Golf Rd.
Rolling Meadows, IL 60008
Phone: 888-783-7546
www.sterlingplumbing.com
Offers ADA-compliant bathroom products

Thibaut Wallcoverings
480 Frelinghuysen Ave.
Newark, NJ 07114
Phone: 973-643-3777
Manufactures wallcovering, borders, and fabric for the home

Tile Council of America, Inc.
100 Clemson Research Blvd.
Anderson, SC 29625
Phone: 864-646-8453
www.tileusa.com
A national trade group, represents tile companies and offers information for consumers, including a handbook on ceramic tile installation

Toto USA
1155 Southern Rd.
Morrow, GA 30260
Phone: 888-295-8134
www.totousa.com
Manufactures toilets and bidets

Saunatec
575 Cokato St. East
Cokato, MN 55321
Phone: 888-780-4427
www.saunatec.com
Manufactures saunas, steam baths, sauna heaters, and other luxury bath items

Seagull Lighting Products, Inc.
301 W. Washington St.
Riverside, NJ 08075
Phone: 856-764-0500
www.seagulllighting.com
Manufactures lighting fixtures

Sherwin-Williams
101 Prospect Ave. NW
10 Midland Building
Cleveland, OH 44114

Warmatowel, Inc., part of The Sussman Lifestyle Group
www.warmatowel.com
Manufactures heated towel bars (See Mr. Sauna.)

Waterworks
60 Backus Ave.
Danbury, CT 06810
Phone: 800-998-2284
www.waterworks.com
Offers luxury plumbing, tile, and furnishings

Whirlpool Corp.
2000 N. M-63
Benton Harbor, MI 49022-2692
Phone: 800-253-1301
www.whirlpool.com
Manufactures major home appliances

Wilsonart International
P.O. Box 6110
Temple, TX 76503-6110
Phone: 800-433-3222
www.wilsonart.com
*Manufactures plastic laminate, solid-surfacing material, and
adhesives for countertops, cabinets, floors, and fixtures*

Velux America
450 Old Brickyard Rd.
P. O. Box 5001
Greenwood, SC 29648
Phone: 800-888-3589
www.velux.com
Manufactures skylight, roof window, and solar energy systems

Villeroy and Boch
3 South Middlesex Ave
Monroe Township, NJ 08831
Phone: 877-505-5350
www.villeroy-boch.com
Manufactures fixtures, fittings, and furniture

Vitra USA
305 Shawnee N. Dr., Ste. 600
Suwanee, GA 30024
Phone: 770-904-6830
www.vitra-usa.com
Manufactures products and accessories for the bath

Wood-Mode Cabinetry
One 2nd St.
Kreamer, PA 17833
Phone: 570-374-2711
www.wood-mode.com
Manufactures custom and semi-custom cabinetry

York Wallcoverings, Inc.
750 Linden Ave.
York, PA 17405
Phone: 800-375-9675
www.yorkwall.com
Manufactures a variety of wallcoverings and borders

glossary OF BATH TERMS

Absorption (light): The energy (wavelengths) not reflected by an object or substance. The color of a substance depends on the wavelength reflected.

Accent lighting: A type of light that highlights an area or object to emphasize that aspect of a room's character.

Accessible design: Design that accommodates persons with physical disabilities.

Accessories: Towel racks, soap dishes, and other items specifically designed for use in the bath.

Adaptable design: Design that can be easily changed to accommodate a person with disabilities.

Ambient light: General illumination that surrounds a room. There is no visible source of the light.

Antiscalding valve (pressure-balancing valve): A single-control fitting that contains a piston that automatically responds to changes in line water pressure to maintain temperature; the value blocks abrupt drop or rise in temperature.

Apron: The front extension of a bathtub that runs from the rim to floor.

Awning window: A window with a single framed-glass panel. It is hinged at the top to swing out when it is open.

Backlighting: Illumination coming from a source behind or at the side of an object.

Barrier-free fixtures: Fixtures specifically designed for disabled individuals who use wheelchairs or who have limited mobility.

Basin: A shallow sink.

Base cabinet: A cabinet that rests on the floor under a countertop or vanity.

Base plan: A map of an existing bathroom that shows detailed measurements and the location of fixtures and their permanent elements.

Bidet: A bowl-shaped fixture that supplies water for personal hygiene. It looks similar to a toilet.

Built-in: A cabinet, shelf, medicine chest, or other storage unit that is recessed into the wall.

Bump out: Living space created by cantilevering the floor and ceiling joists (or adding to a floor slab) and extending the exterior wall of a room.

Candlepower (Cp): The intensity of light measured at the light source.

Cantilever: A structural beam supported on one end. A cantilever can be used to support a small addition.

Casement window: A window that consists of one framed-glass panel that is hinged on the side. It swings outward from the opening at the turn of a crank.

Centerline: The dissecting line through the center of an object, such as a sink.

CFM: An abbreviation that refers to the amount of cubic feet of air that is moved per minute by an exhaust fan.

Clearance: The amount of space between two fixtures, the centerlines of two fixtures, or a fixture and an obstacle, such as a wall. Clearances may be mandated by building codes.

Code: A locally or nationally enforced mandate regarding structural design, materials, plumbing, or electrical systems that states what you can or cannot do when you build or remodel. Codes are intended to protect standards of health, safety, and land use.

Color rendition index (CRI): Measures the way a light source renders color. The higher the index number, the closer colors illuminated by the light source resemble how they appear in sunlight.

Contemporary style: A style of decoration or architecture that is modern and pertains to what is current.

Combing: A painting technique that involves using a small device with teeth or grooves over a wet painted surface to create a grained effect.

Correlated color temperature (CCT): A value assigned to a fluorescent lamp indicating the warmth or coolness of the light it produces.

Dimmer Switch: A switch that can vary the intensity of the light source that it controls.

Downlighting: A lighting technique that illuminates objects or areas from above.

Double-hung window: A window that consists of two framed-glass panels that slide open vertically, guided by a metal or wood track.

Duct: A tube or passage for venting indoor air to the outside.

Enclosure: Any material used to form a shower or tub stall, such as glass, glass block, or a tile wall.

Faux painting: Various painting techniques that mimic wood, marble, and other stones.

Fittings: The plumbing devices that transport water to the fixtures. These can include showerheads, faucets, and spouts. Also pertains to hardware and some accessories, such as towel racks, soap dishes, and toilet-paper dispensers.

Fixture spacing: The amount of space included between ambient light fixtures to achieve an even field of illumination in a given area.

Fixed window: A window that cannot be opened. It is usually a decorative unit, such as a half-round or Palladian-style window.

Fixture: Any fixed part of the structural design, such as tubs, bidets, toilets, and lavatories.

Fluorescent lamp: An energy-efficient light source made of a tube with an interior phosphorus coating that glows when energized by electricity.

Foot-candle (Fc): A unit that is used to measure the brightness produced by a lamp. A foot-candle is equal to one lumen per square foot of surface.

Form: The shape and structure of space or an object.

Full bath: A bath that includes a toilet, lavatory, and bathing fixtures, such as a tub or shower.

Glass blocks: Decorative building blocks made of translucent glass used for non-load-bearing walls to allow passage of light.

Glazing (walls): A technique for applying a thinned, tinted wash of translucent color to a dry undercoat of paint.

Halogen bulb: A bulb filled with halogen gas, a substance that causes the particles of tungsten to be redeposited onto the tungsten filament. This process extends the lamp's life and makes the light whiter and brighter.

Half bath (powder room): A bathroom that contains only a toilet and a sink.

Highlight: The lightest tone in a room.

Incandescent lamp: A bulb that contains a conductive filament through which current flows. The current reacts with an inert gas inside the bulb, which makes the filament glow.

Intensity: Strength of a color.

Jets: Nozzles installed behind the walls of tubs or showers that pump out pressurized streams of water.

Joist: Set in a parallel fashion, these framing members support the boards of a ceiling or a floor.

Lavatory or lav: A fixed bowl or basin with running water and a drainpipe that is used for washing.

Load-bearing wall: A wall that supports a structure's vertical load. Openings in any load-bearing wall must be reinforced to carry the live and dead weight of the structure's load.

Lumen: A term that refers to the intensity of light measured at a light source that is used for general or ambient lighting. Muntins: Framing members of a window that divide the panes of glass.

Palette: A range of colors that complement each other.

Pedestal: A stand-alone lavatory with a basin and supporting column in one piece.

Pocket door: A door that opens by sliding inside the wall, as opposed to a conventional door that opens into a room.

Pressure-balancing valve: Also known as a surge protector or antiscalding device. It is a control that prevents surges of hot or cold water in faucets by equalizing the amounts of hot and cold water pumped out at any time.

Ground-fault circuit interrupter (GFCI): A safety circuit breaker that compares the amount of current entering a receptacle with the amount leaving. If there is a discrepancy of 0.005 volt, the GFCI breaks the circuit in a fraction of a second. GFCIs are required by the National Electrical Code in areas that are subject to dampness.

Grout: A binder and filler applied in the joints between ceramic tile.

218

Proportion: The relationship of one object to another.

Radiant floor heat: A type of heating that is brought into a room via electrical wire or pipes (to carry hot water) that have been installed under the floor. As the pipes or electrical wire heats up, the flooring material warms and heat rises into the room.

Ragging: A painting technique that uses a crumbled piece of cloth to apply or remove small amounts of wet paint to create a pattern or texture.

Reflectance levels: The amount of light that is reflected from a colored surface, such as a tile wall or painted surface.

Roof window: A horizontal window that is installed on the roof. Roof windows are ventilating.

Scale: The size of a room or object.

Schematic: A detailed diagram of systems within a home.

Sconce: A decorative wall bracket, sometimes made of iron or glass, that shields a bulb.

Skylight: A framed opening in the roof that admits sunlight into the house. It can be covered with either a flat glass panel or a plastic dome.

Sight line: The natural line of sight the eye travels when looking into or around a room.

Sliding window: Similar to a double-hung window turned on its side. The glass panels slide horizontally.

Snap-in grilles: Ready-made rectangular and diamond-pattern grilles that snap into a window sash and create the look of a true divided-light window.

Soffit: A boxed in area just below the ceiling and above the upper cabinets.

Space reconfiguration: A design term that is used to describe the reallocation of interior space without adding on.

Sponging: A paint technique that uses a small sponge to apply or remove small amounts of wet paint to create a pattern or texture on a surface.

Spout: The tube or pipe from which water gushes out of a faucet.

Stencil: A design cut out of plastic or cardboard. When paint is applied to the cut-out-area, the design will be reproduced on a surface.

Stud: The vertical member of a framed wall, usually placed every 16 inches on center. A stud provides structural framing and is usually covered with drywall or plywood.

Subfloor: The flooring applied directly to the floor joists on top of which the finished floor rests.

Surround: The enclosure and area around a tub or shower. A surround may include steps and a platform, as well as the tub itself.

Task lighting: Lighting designed to illuminate a particular task, such as shaving.

Tone: The degree of lightness or darkness of a color.

Traditional style: A style of decoration or architecture (typically of the eighteenth and nineteenth centuries) that employs forms that have been repeated for generations without major changes.

Trompe l'oeil: French for "fool the eye." A paint technique that creates a photographically real illusion of space or objects.

True divided-light window: A window composed of multiple glass panes that are divided by and held together by muntins.

Universal design: Products and designs that are easy to use by people of all ages, heights, and varying physical abilities.

Vanity: The countertop and cabinet unit that supports a sink. The vanity is usually included in the bathroom for storage purposes. It may also be used as a dressing table.

Whirlpool: A special tub that includes motorized jets behind the walls of the tub for water massages.

index

photo credits

page 1: Mark Samu, architect: SD Atelier, AIA **page 2:** Mark Samu **page 6:** Jessie Walker **page 8:** Mark Samu **page 11:** courtesy of Ceramic Tiles of Italy **page 12:** Mark Samu, design: Lee Najman Design **page 13:** Beth Singer **page 14:** *left* courtesy of Price Pfister; *right* Mark Samu, builder: Bonacio Construction **page 15:** courtesy of Motif Designs **page 16:** *top* courtesy of DEX Studios; *bottom* Mark Samu, builder: Bonacio Construction **page 17:** Mark Samu, courtesy of Hearst Magazines **pages 18–19:** Jessie Walker **page 20:** davidduncanlivingston.com **pages 22–23:** *both* Minh + Wass, tile & design: Bisazza Mosaica **page 24:** *both* Roy Inman, stylist: Susan Andrews **page 25:** Tony Giammarino/Giammarino & Dworkin **page 26–29:** *all* davidduncanlivingston.com **page 31:** Tony Giammarino/Giammarino & Dworkin **pages 32–33:** davidduncanlivingston.com **page 34:** Mark Lohman, design: Julie Kays Design **page 35:** *both* Nancy Elizabeth Hill, design: Diane Burgoyne Interiors **page 36:** Minh + Wass **pages 38–39:** *all* Mark Lohman, design: Lotto Design Group **pages 40–41:** *all* Mark Lohman, courtesy of Hearst Magazines **page 42:** davidduncanlivingston.com **page 44:** Mark Lohman **page 45:** davidduncanlivingston.com **page 46:** Eric Roth **page 47:** Mark Lohman **page 48:** Eric Roth **page 54:** davidduncanlivingston.com **pages 56:** Mark Lohman, design: Kathryne Designs **page 57:** Mark Lohman, design: Roxanne Packham Design & Michele Hughes Design **page 58:** *all* Mark Lohman, design: Barclay Butera **page 59:** Beth Singer, architect: Dominick Tringali Associates, builder: Custom Homes by DeRocher, Inc. **pages 60–61:** *all* Mark Lohman, design: Harte Brownlee & Assoc. **pages 62–63:** *all* Eric Roth **page 65:** Mark Samu, design Witt Construction

pages 66–67: *all* Mark Lohman, architect: Abramson Tieger **pages 68–69:** *right & top center* design: Kyser Interiors; *bottom left & top left* design: Sally Dixon Design **pages 70–71:** *all* Mark Lohman, design: Dana Jones Design **page 72–73:** *all* Tria Giovan **page 74:** courtesy of Kohler **page 76:** *top* Jessie Walker; *bottom* courtesy of Sloan **page 77:** davidduncanlivingston.com **page 78:** *bottom left* Jessie Walker; *bottom* davidduncanlivingston.com **page 79:** Todd Caverly, builder: G.M. Wild Construction **page 80:** davidduncanlivingston.com **page 81:** courtesy of Kohler **page 82:** Nancy Elizabeth Hill **page 83:** courtesy of VITRA USA **page 85:** Mark Lohman **pages 86–87:** courtesy of Kohler **page 88:** Beth Singer, design: Ausberg Interiors, architect: Young & Young Architects, builder: John Richards Homes **page 90:** Minh + Wass **page 91:** Anne Gummerson, design: Alexander Baer Design **page 92:** *left* Beth Singer, architect: Lubin, Schulz & Skocelas Architects; *right* Beth Singer, design: Robin Wilson Interiors, architect: CBI Architects **page 93:** Anne Gummerson, design: Andre Fontaine, architect: Glen Elg **page 94:** Jessie Walker, design: Jim Rudd **page 95:** Tria Giovan **page 96:** *left* Jessie Walker, architect: George Pappageorge; *right* Tony Giammarino/Giammarino & Dworkin, design/build: Hamilton, Mitchell & King **page 97:** Jessie Walker, design: Paulette O'Reilly Akins & Assoc. **pages 98–99:** *left* Beth Singer, design: NBI Interiors, architect: Angelini & Associates Architects, builder: Christian Tennant Homes; *right* Tria Giovan **page 100:** Anne Gummerson, design: Cristine Wasiak **page 101:** *left* Jessie Walker, architect: David Raino Ogden Architects; *right* Anne Gummerson **page 102:** Anne Gummerson, design: Alexander Baer Design **page 103:** davidduncanlivingston.com **page 104:**

Jessie Walker, design: Neff Kitchens **page 105:** davidduncanlivingston.com **pages 106–107:** Jessie Walker **page 108:** Jessie Walker **page 109:** Beth Singer, design: Kevin McManamon, architects: DesRosiers Architects **pages 110–111:** *all* davidduncanlivingston.com **page 112:** Mark Lohman, design: Taddey & Karlin **page 114:** Nancy Elizabeth Hill, design: Olivia Charney and Olivia Lee **page 115:** Beth Singer, design: Robin Wilson Architects, architect: CBI Architects **pages 116–118:** *all* davidduncanlivingston.com **page 120:** davidduncanlivingston.com **pages 122–123:** *all* davidduncanlivingston.com **page 124:** Mark Samu **page 126:** davidduncanlivingston.com **pages 127–127:** *both* Minh + Wass **page 129:** davidduncanlivingston.com **page 130:** courtesy of Kohler **page 131:** courtesy of Toto **page 132:** courtesy of Kohler **page 133:** Beth Singer, design: Jeffrey King Interiors & Richard Ross Interiors, architect: Bryce, McCalpin & Palazzola Architects, builder: Ray Wallick **page 134:** courtesy of Kohler **page 135:** Tria Giovan **page 136:** davidduncanlivingston.com **page 137:** Nancy Elizabeth Hill, design: Stirling Design Associates **page 138:** davidduncanlivingston.com **page 139:** Beth Singer, design: Jeffrey King Interiors & Richard Ross Interiors, architect: Bryce, McCalpin & Palazzola Architects, builder: Ray Wallick **page 140:** davidduncanlivingston.com **page 141:** Mark Samu **pages 142–143:** courtesy of Armstrong **pages 144–145:** *both* davidduncanlivingston.com **pages 148–149:** *all* Tria Giovan **pages 150–155:** *all* davidduncanlivingston.com **page 156:** Anne Gummerson, design: David Mitchell **page 158:** Mark Lohman **page 159:** Minh + Wass **page 160:** Beth Singer **page 162:** davidduncanlivingston.com **page 163:** Mark Lohman **pages 164–165:** davidduncanlivingston.com

page 166: Minh + Wass **page 167:** Mark Lohman **page 168:** Tony Giammarino/Giammarino & Dworkin **pages 169–172:** davidduncanlivingston.com **page 173:** Jessie Walker **page 174:** davidduncanlivingston.com **page 175:** Jessie Walker **page 176:** *both* Mark Lohman **page 177:** *left* davidduncanlivingston.com; *right* Mark Lohman **pages 178–179:** Minh + Wass **page 180:** Anne Gummerson, design: Gina Fitzsimmons, Fitzsimmons Design Associates **page 181:** davidduncanlivingston.com **page 182:** Nancy Elizabeth Hill **page 183:** davidduncanlivingston.com **pages 184–185:** *right & top left* Mark Samu, builder: T. Michaels Contracting; *bottom left* Mark Samu **pages 186–187:** *all* Mark Samu **pages 188–191:** *all* davidduncanlivingston.com **pages 192–193:** Tria Giovan **page 194:** *bottom left & top* Mark Lohman; *bottom right* davidduncanlivingston.com **pages 195–197:** *all* davidduncanlivingston.com **pages 198–199:** *top & right* Beth Singer; *bottom center* Beth Singer; *bottom left* Beth Singer **page 200:** davidduncanlivingston.com **page 202:** *top both* Mark Samu, design: Chester Winthrop; *bottom* Mark Samu, courtesy of Hearst Magazines **page 203:** *top right & center right* Mark Samu, design: Lucianna Samu Design; *bottom both* Mark Samu, courtesy of Hearst Magazines; *top left* Mark Samu, design: Chester Winthrop **page 208:** courtesy of Kohler **page 209:** courtesy of Merillat **page 210:** courtesy of Moen **page 211:** courtesy of Wood-Mode **page 212:** courtesy of Sonoma **page 213:** courtesy of Lightology **page 214:** Mark Samu, courtesy of Hearst Magazines **page 215:** Mark Samu, courtesy of Hearst Magazines **page 216:** Mark Samu, architect: Len Kurkowski, AIA **page 217:** Mark Samu **page 218:** courtesy of Villeroy & Boch **page 219:** courtesy of Kohler

If you like
The Smart Approach to® Bath Design
take a look at our other Smart Approach books

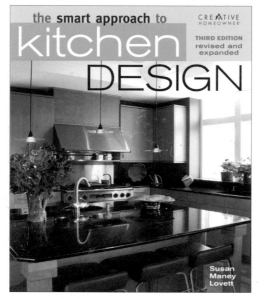

The Smart Approach to® Kitchen Design
How to create a kitchen like a pro. Over
275 photos. 224 pp.; 9¼" x 10⅞"
REVISED AND EXPANDED
BOOK #279952

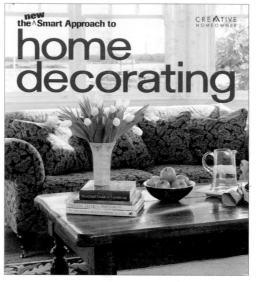

The New Smart Approach to® Home Decorating
How to work with space, color, pattern, and texture. Over 440 photos. 288 pp.; 9" x 10"
BOOK #279672

The Smart Approach to® the Organized Home
How to make the house you have more livable.
Over 350 photos. 208 pp.; 9" x 10"
BOOK #279515

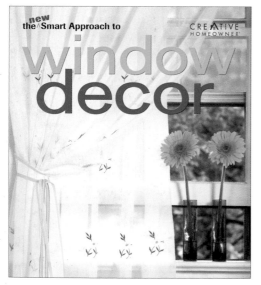

The New Smart Approach to® Window Decor
Plan and select the perfect window treatment.
Over 295 photos & Illustrations. 208 pp.; 9" x 10"
BOOK #279438

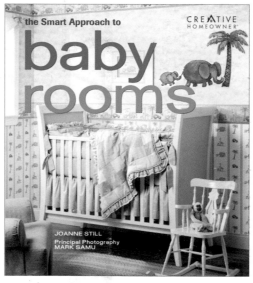

The Smart Approach to® Baby Rooms
Create a beautiful and safe environment for your
baby. Over 330 photos. 208 pp.; 9" x 10"
BOOK #279482

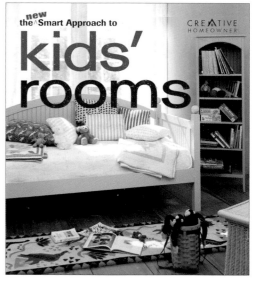

The New Smart Approach to® Kids' Rooms
Learn how to design the perfect room for your
child. Over 300 photos. 208 pp.; 9" x 10"
BOOK #279478

Look for these and other fine **Creative Homeowner** books wherever books are sold.
For more information and to order direct, go to **www.creativehomeowner.com**

APR   2008